Back From Hell

By Dr. Pete Wasko

Dr Pete Wasko

Acknowledgments

Melva Libb, Editor - Thank you so much for your commitment to meeting the deadlines and from taking time out of your busy schedule to complete this work. I have really enjoyed our time of getting to know each other.

Jim Jackson, Cover Design - What happened on the cross is why I made it home from Viet Nam and what happened on the cross is why we have the opportunity for eternal life.

Florence Biros, Publisher - Our kitchen talks have given me more joy and inspiration than you will ever know. I'll never forget the day in your kitchen when you turned around, looked at me and said, "Just name the book 'Back From Hell' because that is where you've been."

Jason and Jessica Wasko - Thank for helping me type this book. You two are much faster than your Dad.

Carla, my wife - I believe the only reason I am where I am today is because of you always being there for me and always believing in me. I look forward to spending the rest of my life with you. I love you!

©2005 Dr. Peter J. Wasko
ISBN 1-884687-54-7

Printed in the United States of America.

Contents

Introduction 4

I Chosen: A Look into the Future 5

    Desire of a Dream 11

    Choices, Choices, Choices 15

II WELCOME TO VIET NAM 19

    Trust Who? 23

    Traumatized 25

    Breaking Point 31

    Rage 37

    A Miracle 41

    Wonder Boy 47

III AM I REALLY HOME? 49

    The Effects of War 53

    The Mental Institution 57

    The Adrenaline Rush 63

    Sick Revenge 67

    Drug Abuse 69

IV MARRIAGE FOR THE WRONG REASON 75

    Honeymoon 79

    My Firstborn 81

    You're Out of Here 83

    Mental Hardness 85

V DELIVERED FROM HELL 87

    The Barn 93

    No Coincidence 97

VI A CHANCE TO START OVER 99

    Blessings From Above 103

    Marriage by God 105

VII IT CAN HAPPEN TO YOU 109

Introduction

Do you feel as though life has not been fair to you? Do you feel as though your life has no meaning or direction? Do you feel stuck in time with no way forward? Have you ever looked back at your life as a child and said "What happened to my life? It hasn't turned out the way I thought it would." Maybe you are sitting there thinking, "Why have all these bad things happened to me? Why was I the victim? Or maybe you are asking yourself, "Why did I do something that caused my own life and someone else's life to be affected in such a negative way? Why have I caused so many people so much pain and anguish?"

I believe we have all asked ourselves at least one of these questions in our lifetime. So I've written this book for you. As you read it I want you to know that there is a personal message on these pages for you. I want you to know that God has you in mind. He wants you to be encouraged and to discover the plan He has for you. So it doesn't matter who you are or how low you have taken your self you can walk away after reading this book and have a completely different outlook on life. Why?— — Because God loves you!!

What is seen was not made out of things which are visible.

I

Chosen: A Look into the Future

Awakened by the sounds of gun fire and explosions, I jolted into a sitting position and looked around. I saw all my buddies in their army uniforms lying on the kitchen floor beside me. The kitchen was filled with darkness and a sense of emptiness. Even though my friends were right there with me, the room felt like it was void of any life except my own. There were no chairs, table, stove or refrigerator. The entire room was draped in only two colors black and grey. The cabinets appeared to be painted black in the center of each door and shaded to a light grey on the outer edges. The kitchen was filled with a misty blue haze and the smell of gun smoke. I wondered why my buddies were not disturbed by the impact of the terrifying sounds

As I jumped to my feet and strained to see all around, I murmured to myself, I don't understand! Why are my friends not waking up? All this noise could awaken a deaf man! Peering through the haze, I looked to my left and saw a large window mounted on a black wall. Slowly I eased my self toward the window, constantly looking back hoping one of my friends would wake up. When I got to the window I stood in awe of what was before my eyes, an intense battle between two armies made visible by the vivid colors of the explosions of rockets,

e. The sound of the battle vibrated the walls
r and closer the bright flashes and the deaf-
. I felt the presence of evil and danger press-
ely. Then I turned and realized an angelic
g beside me.

grabbed me by my wrist with firmness, yet
s of a woman, and tugged on me to go with
her. "You've been chosen, Pete. You've been chosen. You have
been chosen to live!" she said as she continued to whisk me
away from the scene of horror.

When I turned my head and looked back, I saw all my
buddies still asleep on the floor of the abandoned home where
we were to spend the night and knew they would all be killed.
Snapping my head toward the angelic being I tried to resist
her insistent tug. As she hovered just above the floor and
flowed in the direction she was trying to take me, my resis-
tance was no contest for her strength. Guiding me out of the
jaws of sure death, she repeated over and over, "You have
been chosen, Pete. You have been chosen. You have been chosen to live."

Although I was so frightened I could hardly move, I managed to awaken enough to scramble out of bed and run to my
mother's room as fast as my little seven-year-old legs could
carry me. "Mom!" I cried out. "Mom! I had that dream again!
What does it mean?"

She took me into her arms and tried to comfort me. "I have
no idea what the dream means, Pete. Come on; let's go down-
stairs until you calm down. Let's get the Bible" She held me
close to her on the living room couch in our Farrell, Pennsylvania apartment as I described the details of the dream.

"Mom," I asked her "what does the Lord's Prayer mean?"
(I knew the Lord's Prayer and the Twenty-third Psalm inside
and out. I had learned them in first grade. My teacher, Miss
McGee, told us, "I don't care what else you will know when
you leave here, but you WILL know the Twenty-third Psalm
and the Lord's Prayer.") "Mom, 'the valley of shadow of death,'
what does that mean? The Lord's Prayer, what does all this

mean?"

Tears of helplessness welled up in my mother's eyes. "I don't know, Pete. I don't know what they mean."

Nevertheless, every night before I went to bed and every morning when I awoke, I recited these two important Scriptures, even in my adult years.

I dreamed this same war dream repeatedly until I was eleven years old. *I had no idea this dream would become a reality in future years.*

This was not my only encounter with abnormal dreams or visions. Just prior to having this dream for the first time, I attended a vacation Bible school at a church a couple of miles away from home. Some of my mother's friends who lived in our same building knew we didn't have a car, so they insisted on providing transportation for my oldest brother and me to go to the church along with their sons. While at Bible school one day our teacher gave each of us a picture of Jesus to color. I colored His hair yellow. When the teacher looked at my finished work of art, she said, "Pete, Jesus was a Jew. He had brown hair."

I replied, "But, teacher, as I was looking at the picture right after you gave it to me, I saw Jesus' hair glowing bright yellow like the sun. So I colored His hair as I saw it."

On another occasion at vacation Bible school, the same teacher distributed pictures of a cross and once again I colored mine yellow.

"Pete, why did you color the cross yellow?" she asked. "The cross was made out of a tree. It was brown."

Again, I explained, "As I was looking at the cross, it was glowing bright yellow like the sun, so I colored it the way I saw it."

As I advanced in my ability to read I often opened our huge family Bible and copied on paper the words which were printed in red. I knew those were the words spoken by Jesus so they had to be important.

As I reflect back at these times, I can see that Jesus was at work in my life. I don't know why I was chosen, but I was!

And it seems that no matter what the situation, through the Holy Spirit or however God chose, I have been protected.

For example, one day when I was eight or nine I went to a place where I should not have been. A place called Rocky Springs. I walked by myself about three miles through swamps and woods to get there. On several occasions our family went there to play in the creek and have picnics on the picnic tables with strings of light bulbs hanging over them..

This particular time, as young boys often do, I lost track of time and before I new it, it was dusk. Well, not only did I know I would not make it back through the swamps and woods in the dark, I was afraid to attempt it. So, what did I do? I chose to cross the bridge over the creek to the main road and hitch hike home.

As I walked down the road and approached a farm house, two dogs, a German Shepherd and a Collie, ran toward me, barking with destruction in their eyes. They were self-appointed protectors of their kingdom and I was an intruder. I knew I was their supper!

In an instant, two thoughts came to my mind. A picture which hung on the wall of our home of Daniel petting lions in the lions' den and a small red Salvation Army pocket Bible I carried in my back pocket. I figured that if God could save Daniel from the lions, He could save me from my attackers.

As quickly as possible I pulled the Bible out of my pocket and began to read out loud as I walked. I refused to take my eyes off the words in that small book, determined to stay focused on the Word and scared to lift my head to see what was going to happen next.

As I heard the barking come closer and closer, my heart was about to pound its way out of my little chest. Out of the corner of my eye, I could see the dogs enter my peripheral vision. Raising my head, I looked square into their threatening eyes, even though they were only about three feet away from me.

In a split second, they skidded to a halt, turned around and ran for home as though they had seen a ghost. I was so excited! I knew somehow God had protected me from what had appeared to be a very dangerous situation. For a moment I thought I had escaped without any harm, but what happened next was not a good thing.

A white car approached, so I stuck out my thumb to hitch a ride home. The car stopped and I opened the door. Instead of getting in, I FROZE! To my surprise, the driver was my mother. But – we didn't own a car! I knew what was to come next because Mom had beaten my butt so many times for disobeying!

Finally, managing to speak, I asked, "Mom, where'd you get the car?"

"Get … in … the … car!"

"OK." Did I have a choice? I learned later she'd just bought the car that day. During the short ride home I tried to divert her attention and receive some compassion by describing the dog scene, but to no avail.

Mom responded, "I figured, since it was almost dark and nobody seemed to know where you were, you had to have done something stupid like venture out to Rocky Springs on your own. You know, when you get home you're getting your butt beat. And you're grounded!" The story of my life! Chosen and protected by God from those dogs just as He had spared Daniel from the lions, but not spared from my mother's wrath! I thought, *God and my mother must think alike! They both feel I deserve discipline.* I was not the easiest child to raise.

On several different occasions my mother took me to stay at her sisters' and brothers' homes to see if they could get me under control, but I always ended up back home. (Today I am grateful for my mother's firm discipline. Most parents are afraid to discipline their children. They don't want to admit it, but their kids rule them!)

> *Faith is the substance of things hoped for, the evidence of things not seen.*

Pete, home on leave at age seventeen.

Desire o

I believe that every child drea⸺ ⸺y want to become when they grow up. Chil⸺ ⸺ed with imaginations that help them soar above ⸺ ⸺e difficult and frightening times they may encounter. When rough times hit the home front, a child's imagination and his dreams will carry him into tomorrow to escape from his current troubles.

I was one of those unfortunate kids who lived in an unstable home situation. My father was an alcoholic who frequently came home drunk and started fights with my mother. Often he was taken to jail for his violence. As most children do, I dealt with each traumatic circumstance by allowing my thoughts to take me into another world. I dreamed I would become a doctor. Oh, how I wanted to be a doctor!

At that time Dr. Kildare and Ben Casey were famous television characters that devoted their lives to helping people put their broken life situations back together. I spent many hours imagining I was a Dr. Kildare who helped people who were hurting as much as I was.

There was a Murphy's department store about a mile and a half from home. My brothers and I often walked there to look around and buy treats. One day I found a doctor's medical bag in the toy department. I mowed lawns for ten cents a lawn and saved the money I earned to buy a Ben Casey doctor shirt and that toy doctor's bag.

When I played cowboys and Indians with my buddies, we always set up a "med tent" where we took our wounded and,

played cowboys wearing my Ben

at everyone call me "Dr. Wasko."

d with my doctor career that my mother

ily physician and told him, "All Pete can talk

oming a doctor. I've just got to find a way to get

to see what goes on in a hospital. Maybe if he sees

t goes on there, he'll stop talking about it."

A few days later, Mom and I met the doctor in the emergency room and began our hospital tour from there. He took me with him on his rounds to see some of his patients. As we walked down one of the long corridors, he came to an abrupt stop, looked down at me and asked, "Pete, why do you want to be a doctor?"

"Because I love people and want to help them get better," I responded without hesitation. He guided me into a cubicle where there were empty chairs and motioned for me to sit down.

"Pete, I can tell you have the same sensitivity for people that I have. But you need to know you can't help everyone. Sometimes patients die. That's very hard to take. When this happens, you can't blame yourself."

His words shook the core of my little self. *Die! There must be ways and methods not yet thought of that will make all people better!* All the way home I was silent, thinking about what it must be like to be a doctor and have a patient die. I couldn't imagine what that would be like, so I didn't! Instead I focused my fantasies on becoming the best doctor on earth, getting everyone well just like the TV doctors did. None of my patients would die!

Times were really tough back then. We were living on relief {known as welfare or public assistance today}. I remember walking with my mother and my older brother Paul to the American Legion building where they distributed food to the people on relief. We would pick up a pound or two of rice, a block of cheese, a block of lunch meat, flour, peanut butter and a can of pork and gravy. We carried them to our three bedroom apartment in a government assisted housing project in Farrell, Pennsylvania.

Not only did my mother have to rear her three sons on her own, she didn't know how! Like my mother, most mothers and fathers don't know how to bring up their kids because their parents didn't know what they were doing when they raised them. There were no instruction books or owner's manuals that "came with the package." Plus, all kids are different. Siblings can live under the same situation, be cared for by the same parents under the same roof and beat with the same belt, yet see and interpret what goes on in completely different ways.

Parents often look upon each child according to the way he or she behaves. Unfortunately I acted like my father, which caused my mother to say, "Pete, you are just like your father." If I heard it once, I heard it said a thousand times.

Her words not only hurt me. They confused me. In my little brain I knew my father hurt my mother physically and made her cry a lot. On more than one occasion she called the police and had him put in jail. I concluded, *If my mother doesn't like my dad and has him put in jail, then she must not like me. If she had the chance, would she have me put in jail?*

I loved my mother very much and always tried to please her by hugging her and telling her how much I loved her. I ironed my clothes, cleaned the house – did almost anything to get her approval. Although we often sat together and talked about the things in the Bible, always in the back of my mind I continued to believe, *She wants me in jail.*

I wanted to be a doctor, not a jailbird! I knew I wasn't any angel, but neither was I "just like my father"! *You really want me in jail?* I'd ponder as I lay on my bed at night. *I've never hit you. I never drank alcohol. I mean, come on, Mom! I'm not even ten years old and you're saying I'm going to be a jailbird? Can't you see what I'm trying to become?*

Was I like my father? Yes! But only in the respect that I was very, very stubborn and could not be controlled. With her words indelibly burned in my mind, the older I became the more rebellious I turned out to be. Often I said to myself, *You think my father is bad? Well, you haven't seen anything yet. I'm going to make my daddy look like a Boy Scout!* My dream of becoming a doctor and helping others out of their sickness and pain had been stolen.

Did my mother have any intention of destroying my dreams? Of course not! When I was eleven, she managed to buy me a set of Reader's Digest medical encyclopedias. My rebellion came from my immature and undeveloped thought responses because my mind worked on a different wave length from hers. I had the mind of a child and she had the mind of an adult.

> *Do not be decieved;*
> *Bad company corrupts good morals*

Choices, Choices, Choices

What is your greatest power? Think about this for a minute. Is it your personality? financial status? muscle strength? self control? body odor? (Just kidding!) Is it our Heavenly Father, Jesus or the Holy Spirit? I believe the answer is the same for everyone. It is the God-given power to choose!

You have the power to choose whether or not you get involved with cigarettes, drugs, alcohol, recreational sex or gambling, just a few of the destructive choices people make. Constructive choices are the opposite of the ones just mentioned. You may not realize it, but you even have the right to choose whether you will be rich or poor. What you do with your life is your choice.

When I was eleven years old I chose to start smoking cigarettes and drinking alcohol with my closest companion, my cousin Frank. His mother and mine were sisters. His father and mine were brothers. Our fathers both enjoyed drinking alcohol and abusing their wives.

I believe I started to drink alcohol to ease the pain caused by my father coming home drunk screaming at my mother and even beating her. For me alcohol was a form of self-medication, just as people often self-medicate themselves with drugs, chocolate, work or any other form of over indulgence hoping to alter their painful state of mind to one more tolerable.

When Frank and I were thirteen, we were hired by the same printing company. Our first summer job! I added burglarizing the store across the street to my list of bad choices. No one forced me to do any of these things. No one twisted my arm and said, "You must do this!"

As a matter of fact, my cousin Frank chose not to break into the store. He said it was wrong. "There'll be consequences to pay, Pete, and I'm not willing to pay them. Besides, it's just wrong and you're stupid for even thinking of doing such a thing." His was a GOOD CHOICE!

When I was fifteen, I first saw "her." She was beautiful! I'll never forget the first time I laid eyes on her. We were roller skating. I watched her gracefully glide past the other skaters to the beat of the music. Not only was she beautiful, she had a body to match her looks. Her eyes were filled with life and fire.

I invited her to be my skating partner and she accepted. We talked all evening long as we skated. After this first night together, we both knew we had to see each other again, even though she was four years older than I, married and already mother of a little girl.

Again, my cousin Frank did not approve of my choice. He insisted over and over again, "Pete, this is all wrong! You shouldn't be seeing a married woman!"

I assured him, "It's okay, Frank. Her husband is in the Air Force. And they're getting a divorce anyway." Another BAD CHOICE!

After we had dated for about a year, I arrived home one afternoon just as the phone began to ring. "Hello?" It was Aunt Twila, my mothers sister "Mom isn't home, but I'll tell her you called."

"I didn't call to talk to your mom, Pete. I called to talk to you about your married girlfriend."

I shuddered when I heard her speak truth. In futile defense I retorted, "You need to mind your own business! Stay out of my life!"

"If you don't tell your mother, I will!" she threatened. I said a few choice words and hung up.

Only minutes later my mother walked in the door just as

the phone rang again. You guessed it. I was exposed! The six months that followed were not pleasant. And the situation grew worse for me when the girl's husband came home. I found out they were not getting a divorce, nor were they separated. I decided to drink more and more to cover up my frustration and disillusionment.

At the end of eleventh grade my brother Glenn squealed on me for drinking all the time. My mother, in an effort to get me under control, tried to ground me.

"No one is going to tell me what to do!" I shouted. To escape others' attempts to control my life I decided to quit school and join the Marines. However, since I was only seventeen I had to have my parent's signature on the dotted line before the military would accept me. My mother would not sign for me to go into the Marines so I joined the Army. BAD CHOICE!

I enlisted in the Army to be a Military Policeman, figuring I'd try to do something right for a change. *Yeah, I've done a few bad things*, I reasoned, *but there must be some good in me* somewhere. My mother was pleased that I was going be a military policeman.

After completing my basic training, I was told I was on my way to Fort Knox, Kentucky, to be trained as a recon scout in the armory division. I was shocked.

"That can't be true!" I exclaimed to no one in particular. "I enlisted for military police school."

My sergeant laughed when he heard my outburst. "You're a seventeen-year-old drop out, Private Wasko! When you enlisted, you came in RA (regular army), unassigned. So the army can do anything they want with you." I went to Fort Knox and trained in the field of armored recon. NO CHOICE!

We learned everything there was to know about a variety of weapons, including the fifty-caliber anti-aircraft machine gun, M-60 machine gun, forty-five caliber hand gun, M-79 grenade launcher and the LAW (light artillery weapon). I was taught to drive an M-114 light armored vehicle. I enjoyed all the power I had at my disposal.

However, one problem remained. I was fully trained for

battle, but still only seventeen years old. So the army sent me to Germany, not a good place for me. The first night after my arrival, in October of 1967, I went AWOL (absent without leave) with a guy from West Virginia. Bad Choice! He told me he was going to teach me how to drink. I laughed.

On one ocassion during an inspection at Camp Gates, a border patrol camp, a high ranking officer walked up to me and asked me what my job was. I guess he asked me because I only had on a shirt, pants and boots. There was a blizzard taking place with subzero temperatures. I said, "I am a "Machs nichts" man (makes no difference man)." He wasn't too happy with me. Bad Choice! The rest of the men were dressed in winter clothing and had weapons. They wouldn't allow me to have a weapon. I was in trouble most of the time for drinking and spent about half of my time shoveling ashes on the hill leading up to the camp.

On January 7, 1968, the day I turned eighteen, I volunteered for Viet Nam and talked my drinking buddy from West Virginia into volunteering with me. Bad Choice! I did not receive my orders for Nam until June of '68. However, from January until that time, I was in a lot of trouble. As a result of my continued bad choices, I was sent for psychiatric evaluation and was soon in the process of being kicked out of the army on the grounds of "unable to adapt to military life." Somehow the incident was dropped and I was able to continue with my career in the army.

As I look back on this time of my life, I believe God continued to protect me from a dishonorable discharge because He had greater plans for me. So, He protected me in spite of my series of bad choices. As you will see, my bad choices didn't end there.

II

WELCOME TO VIET NAM

I'll never forget the day I arrived in Viet Nam. As our jumbo jet came to a complete stop and we stood up to exit I didn't know what to expect. Would the enemy be shooting at us as we got off the plane? I was only eighteen. Scared, yet excited, but totally uneducated. I paused at the door of the plane and sniffed the air.

"What's that awful smell?" I asked. I soon learned about the open sewage in that area combined with the smell of death which penetrated the atmosphere of the whole country.

We were all taken to the processing center and then sent to different units. I was informed that I was going to the 11th Armored Calvary in Xuan Loc. The 11th was an armored unit consisting of tanks and M-113 armored personnel carriers. After I arrived at my assigned destination, I went through more schooling, this time to learn how to survive in the jungle and how to spot and disarm booby traps.

Then came the big test, my first ambush patrol. I had no idea that what I was about to experience that night would begin to alter my sleep patterns for the next twenty years!

We left base camp toward evening to set up the ambush. On the way to our position, I noticed I was the next to the last man. Because I'd seen so many war movies and cowboy movies when I was a little boy, my mind was running wild! I knew the last man in the patrol got picked off first, then the next, and so on. So I kept looking behind me to make sure the last man was still all right, all the time wondering, *Are they going to pick me off? Are they going to hit us? From the left? The right? From behind? Where are they going to hit us from?* I was scared to death! *If they do hit me, do I shoot back?* The thought of killing someone sent a chill up my spine.

Once we'd reached our destination, a sergeant placed us about six to eight feet apart and instructed us to stand guard for two hours, and then awaken the other guy to guard while we slept for two hours. I thought, *There's no way I'm going to sleep tonight!*

About two in the morning I crawled over to Miller, the guy next to me, and followed my instructions, talking to him to make sure he was awake.

"Miller," I whispered, "when were you born? What day is this? Are you sure you're awake?"

"Yeah, I'm awake. I'm awake!"

"Miller, whatever you do, don't fall asleep or we'll all be killed! I can't sleep anyway, so if you want me for anything, I'll stay here with you."

"Naw, I'm okay. I'm okay."

I returned to my position with great hesitation. No way was I going to be able to sleep. Every nerve in my body was filled with adrenaline. Sleep was an unfeasible thought.

I lay as quietly as possible for about twenty minutes, trying not to make a sound, trying to hear Miller breathing. I couldn't hear even the slightest sound. Something just wasn't right! *He must be sleeping,* I thought, and tried to get his attention without making too much noise. But no luck. My mind was racing with the most terrifying thoughts of what could have happened to Miller.

Was I next? Did a gook sneak up on him and stab him with a knife? Now is he hiding over there, waiting to get me? {I believe we called all Vietnamese people gooks so our conscious minds would not associate killing them with the reality of having killed another human being.} I didn't know whether to crawl back over where Miller was or stay put until morning. If something were to go wrong, I had no idea how to get back to the base camp. *What if they capture me? Will they make me a prisoner of war? Or because I'm only a private, will they torture then kill me?* Finally I couldn't stand the suspense any longer and somehow mustered enough nerve to crawl over to him. As I approached his area, I could see the outline of his body lying on the ground curled into a ball.

"Miller!" I whispered. No response. "Miller!" Again no response.

Mentally I cried out with horror, He's dead! ...or is he just sleeping? I didn't want to touch him. I'd never touched a dead person, so I put my face right next to his and whispered louder, "Miller!"

He jumped up. "What? What? What? Is everything okay?" I thought I was going to die when he leaped up! Grabbing his shoulders, I shook him, rasping, "What are you doing? You could've had us all killed! Next time you fall asleep on ambush patrol, you're mine, buddy! I'll kill you!"

That night I realized I couldn't depend on anyone but myself. If I was going to have any chance at all of making it back home alive, it had to be up to me. I vowed, *I'm not going to die because of someone else's mistake.*

Within a week we were shipped out to the field, a combat area. As a gunner on an armored personnel carrier, I was under a sergeant who was serving his third tour of duty in Viet Nam. He'd been wounded eight times and had been awarded three silver and two bronze stars for bravery. He just loved being there. To me, he was an Audie Murphy! I respected this man even though I'd already seen him kill several Vietnamese "by accident."

One day while we were on a mail run, our commander was trying to talk to the sarge on the radio. The sarge couldn't hear him, so he stopped on the road. As we were sitting there, our driver grabbed his M-16 rifle and pulled the trigger to see if it was loaded. The M-16 fired just as a few lambrettas filled with people were going by. (You've probably seen these lambrettas in Oriental movies. They look like little motor bikes shaped like double layered station wagons on three wheels.)

Well, the driver tried to get the sergeant's attention to tell him what had happened, but failed, so my sergeant thought those people were firing at us. The next thing I knew, our sergeant opened fire on them with a fifty caliber machine gun. In moments there wasn't much left of the lambrettas or the people who had been riding on them, and the one-sided skirmish was over.

I was surprised that seeing the dead people didn't bother me. But war was too new to me and the incident didn't seem real.

Our commanding officer yelled over the radio, "What's the firing about, Sergeant?"

"False alarm, Sir." He looked at me, smiled and shrugged his shoulders.

I knew this sergeant was a man who could teach me how to stay alive. He'd never go to sleep on me either! I respected that man, even though he collected ears from dead gooks and carried them with him as trophies. The ears didn't seem real to me either. Too much was happening too fast for me to judge someone for what they did, even for collecting human ears. I mean, come on, this guy was still alive, wasn't he? That's all that mattered. I didn't care what he'd done. Besides, I wasn't with him when he collected them.

Fear, tension, sleepless nights and unpredictable days. Welcome to Viet Nam!

Trust Who?

One day while we were on a search and destroy mission, Sarge asked me, "Do you smoke?"

I boasted, "I've been smoking since I was eleven years old!"

He handed me a pipe filled with marijuana and said, "I'll bet you've never had anything like this before."

My whole body tensed. *I thought he meant cigarettes, not weed! Now what am I going to do?* Here was a guy who was going to protect me and possibly save my life, someone I really respected. I didn't want him mad at me or thinking I was a weakling. Refusing his offer might jeopardize my opportunity to learn from his experiences. After all, he'd been in this kind of situation for almost three years, and had been wounded eight times. Three silver stars, a couple bronze stars – this man knew how to stay alive!

My inner hesitation and wrestling with my conscience came from the fact that I'd always told myself that if I ever caught anyone smoking that stuff, I would turn them in. But this was different. A matter of life and death. *I don't dare turn him down,* I reasoned. *Getting high is just in your head anyway.* So I grabbed hold of that pipe called a bowl, and dragged on it like I would have dragged on a cigarette, holding the smoke in my lungs like I'd seen him do.

I began to smoke with Sarge and the others every day, laughing as I told them, "Man, getting high is all in your head! This stuff doesn't affect me!"

They were laughing, too, because I was the one who was

really getting totally ripped, high, without realizing the effect it was having on me, at least not until I caught myself eating everything in sight. I was even savoring C- rations and nasty food like canned ham and eggs and pork slices. Usually we wouldn't eat half that stuff because it tasted so bad. Here I was, chowing down like those rations were being served at home for a Thanksgiving Day dinner!

A few days later, my sergeant was taken out of the field against his will and sent home, because he had jungle rot so bad his feet would not heal. By that time, it was too late for me to escape the drug trap. I was already captive to the contents of that pipe.

A new inner struggle began. *Would I be able to trust my new sergeant?* There was no time to contemplate the trust factor. We were moving closer to the Cambodian border to a place called Loc Ninh. My new track commander acted scared. He didn't have that confident look in his eyes I was used to seeing in my previous sergeant. I didn't trust him.

> # *Your thoughts are the beginning of your reality.*

Traumatized

When people are traumatized physically, psychologically or both, they are usually driven so far away from their reality they rarely find their way back to their original state. But what traumatizes one person may not affect another, even though their situations may be similar. Nevertheless, when people are traumatized they are never the same again.

On our way to our assigned destination, the convoy of which we were a part received word from headquarters that enemy activity had been detected ahead of us. We were soon to face action for the first time.

As we bounced down the rutted road in our track, an M-113 APC {armored personnel carrier} manned by four or five men, a sudden small puff of smoke would emit from the tree line, followed by a little hollow sound that reminded me of the tubes we used at home to set off fireworks. Next I'd see an explosion near us and then close to another nearby vehicle. The enemy was trying to hit our convoy with mortars.

Most of the time we didn't sleep inside the track. If a rocket-propelled grenade, better known as an RPG, hit an APC it would be a sure death for anyone inside. Yet up to that point I'd thought Viet Nam was kind of neat, consisting of riding around in the jungle, looking for the enemy but never seeing them. I'd never seen anyone wounded or killed but the enemy.

Once we arrived at our destination, we were in contact with the enemy at least once a day for twenty-two days in a row. Imagine! I was only eighteen years old, had only been in Viet Nam for a few weeks and had already engaged in several firefights with the enemy, shooting and killing other human beings to stay alive.

We couldn't see the enemy most of the time. But we did experience frantic, wild barrages of noisy displays of fire power. Then one day all that changed.

We captured two prisoners who were put on the same APC (armored personnel carrier) I was on. I was sitting on the back deck, my adrenaline pumping.

"You guard the prisoners, Wasko. If they try to escape, shoot 'em!"

Man! Was the adrenaline pumping! I kept my .45 hand gun aimed toward them, but I was petrified. The prisoners were sitting directly across from me. I saw fear gripping their faces and terror in their eyes. Without warning, the sergeant who was our track commander put a vice grip around the neck of one of them, took the cigar out of his own mouth and began to burn our captive's eyes out.

The helpless prisoner screamed and fought to free himself from the painful terrifying death grip, so the sergeant threw him to the ground. "Run over him," he commanded our driver who maneuvered our thirteen ton vehicle across the man's body without hesitation. Unfortunately the second prisoner never lived to tell about his capture either.

I'd never seen anyone tortured before. As I witnessed the attitudes of my fellow soldiers in action, I was scared. *What's going on?* I tried to interpret what I was witnessing. *Am I in the real world or in hell? If I turn these guys in, what will happen to me? How am I going to get out of this mess?* I knew I was in an impossible position and couldn't escape. *Here I am, half way around the world in a war, and I still have eleven months left ... if I make it that long!*

I observed that I was the only one who was upset over this horrifying act of unjustified murder. Everyone else must have been desensitized already to this type of atrocity. They acted as if the sarge had just stepped on an ant or some other form of annoying insect. *Oh God!* I cried inside. *What just happened? Is this just a bad nightmare? Did I really see what I think I saw? This really didn't happen ... or did it? I don't know what's going on! I can't get a grip on reality here! THIS CAN'T BE REAL!*

One day we pulled to the left of the village Loc Ninh that we were supposed to protect. However, in Viet Nam you never knew who the enemy was. I was the right rear gunner on Track One Zero. To our surprise, the village people opened fire on us from the front and right sides. Before we had time to respond, the enemy opened fire from the left side as well. As we were caught in this u-shaped ambush, the enemy tried to close off the back side to completely surround us.

Several of our men had already been hit, including an infantry unit that was in our area. We pulled three of the wounded into our track. One was lifeless; another had a large hole in his side and was screaming with pain. The third lay face down. From his waist to his ankles he looked like raw meat. He struggled to turn and assess the extent of his wounds and screamed, "I'm going home! I'm going home to Texas!"

More wounded men were pulled onto another armored personnel carrier. Our responsibility was to break through enemy lines and get the wounded to safety. As we broke through enemy lines, I could see our adversaries everywhere! Nearly hysterical, I shot at them with my M-60 machine gun, and in a split second I saw an intense flash of light and heard a loud explosion in front of me. A blast of heat hit my head and right hand.

I stared at my burning hand, bloody and with metal protruding. I realized the heat I'd felt in my head indicated that I'd been wounded there also. But I knew I had to keep fighting if I intended to stay alive

Somehow we reached the medivac helicopters, better known as dust off choppers, and loaded the wounded on the choppers. Someone noticed my wounds and ordered, "Soldier, get on the chopper!" I refused.

After the helicopters took off, we turned around and headed back into the fight. Soon after we entered the battle zone the encounter ended.

We stayed in the jungle for the night. Some of the other men picked the metal out of my head and hand and cleaned me up as much as possible. The next day, when we returned to where our main unit was set up, my wounds were cleaned and dressed by the medics before they tagged me to be air lifted to a hospital. The shrapnel imbedded in my hand and fingers caused swelling that cut off circulation in the ring finger of my right hand. In fact, my finger was so swollen I couldn't even see the ring I wore. A friend had made it out of a fifty cent piece and gave it to me for good luck. My finger which was turning black had been saved by that good luck ring.

Some mechanic friends of mine offered to solve my problem "if I was man enough." Knowing we were short handed for combat, I stood up and walked with them to their work area. One man grabbed hold of my finger and squeezed it while the other began to cut the ring with a hack saw. Once the ring was off, I returned to the medics and announced, "I don't want to get dusted off. I want to go back out to the field. I'm okay."

They checked my hand and saw the ring was off and my hand wasn't seriously wounded. But they did find a small piece of metal remaining in my knuckle and used a pair of needle-nosed pliers to remove it, then sent me on my way.

As I nursed my sore finger and thought back over the incident, I received the answer to my persistent questioning. *Yes, what I'd seen and experienced was real. And it WAS hell!*

One day we were sent to an area very close to the Cambodian border. A spotter plane accompanied us to keep us informed of any enemy activity in front of us, their location and whether they were set up to hit us. Our instructions were, "Don't open fire on them until they fire first." But the moment they fired, all hell broke loose! A rocket-propelled grenade hit the track next to ours killing three out of the four men.

This was not a normal fire fight where the enemy hits you and quickly leaves. Their goal was to wipe us out! More and more of our men were hit. Mass chaos! It was apparent that we didn't stand much of a chance, so our commanding officer called in an air strike for support.

We had exhausted almost all of our ammo, so we backed our tracks together to form a circle. As the enemy ran toward us, I was on the ground firing the LAW, a weapon that resembles a little bazooka, into the advancing North Vietnamese regular army troops. When the jets arrived, they dropped napalm bombs all around our circle. (A napalm bomb is a bomb filled with jelled gasoline that explodes on impact covering anything and everything in its path with burning gasoline.) I can still see the enemy running and on fire. A sure death situation for all fifty of us ended with abruptness, with only seven left who were still walking. Three of us continued to guard while the other four tended to the wounded and dead, carrying them to the helicopters to be evacuated to the hospital.

I still remember watching them pick up body parts and the dead. A rocket-propelled grenade had hit the track next to ours, killing three of the four men. The explosion removed the driver's head. I can't begin to describe the effect of seeing the charred human flesh and exposed internal organs of those men. It was another day in hell!

A day that will be etched in my mind forever: the cries for help, the screaming of the wounded in pain, the sound of "Medic! Medic! Medic!" ringing through the air, and the roar of jets over our heads as they saved our lives; the enemy charging and dying in front of us in their moment of glory but in horrifying defeat.

The gunner on the track next to me survived and made it home. To this day I still talk to him from time to time but the only part of him that made it home intact was his body. He is still suffering mentally because his mind is still in HELL!

Imagine! I was only eighteen years old, had only been in Viet Nam for a few weeks and had already engaged in several firefights with the enemy, shooting and killing other humans in order to stay alive.

> *We become what we think about.*

Pete Wasko. Here I am near the Cambodian border. The weapon is a grenade launcher. I am behind my gun shield which also had an M60 machine gun mounted to it. I was eighteen years old at the time and had already been wounded once when I caught some metal from a rocket propelled grenade (RPG).

Breaking Point

Our job was to go into an area where we knew the enemy was hiding, get them to open fire on us and then call in an air strike or the artillery. The type of war games our commanders appeared to be playing with us made no sense at all. They didn't care about my life or about any of the regular ground units who were fighting and dying in this so-called "police action." I thought, *Now, what kind of sense does this make? We're in a war, so I want to WIN! So why are we still here when we could have ended this war in ninety days or less?*

As you can see, a destructive pattern was building in my mind from the first time on ambush patrol where I didn't trust anyone. Because of all that had happened in the past few months, my thinking was becoming more and more distorted and deranged. I had become a survivor with an attitude, a very rebellious soldier. I was certain that no one could take care of me as well as me. No way could I trust the men in charge of the war because it seemed as though they really didn't care. There were only a few of us that could count on each other in a jam.

A few days after a buddy and I got back from R&R {rest and recuperation for seven days} in Sydney, Australia, I was moved from a gunner position to a driver. We had two new guys for gunners, one who had been in the field for a few months and the other for only a couple of weeks. My track commander was a man with whom I did not get along with because I felt he wasn't capable of doing his job well. He seemed scared and was always making stupid little mistakes. It's usually the little mistakes that cost people their lives.

One warm balmy night while on ambush patrol, one of our gunners told me he spotted some gooks in front of our command track. He handed me the night scope and I confirmed the enemy activity. When I told our sergeant, his response was, "There's nothing I can do about it until they open fire on us."

At that moment, I LOST IT! I grabbed him, yanked the headphones from his head and shoved him out of my way. I radioed the sergeant of the command track and told him, "The gooks are right in front of your track setting up for the kill! You need to open fire!"

He radioed back, "I have to call headquarters and get permission to fire. Don't do anything until I tell you to." I pulled my headphones off and threw them down so I couldn't hear the command sergeant anymore and prepared to open fire. I grabbed the fifty caliber machine gun, aimed it into the area where I'd seen the enemy and pushed the butterfly trigger. Nothing happened! Our inept sergeant hadn't even loaded a round of ammo in the chamber! I grabbed the loading lever, pulled it back, aimed the gun and fired. When I fired, so did everyone else.

When the barrage stopped, my command sergeant screamed, "Wasko, if we don't have a body count, I'm going to court marshal you!"

As we edged our vehicle forward, my gunner yelled, "Pete! To your right!"

I turned just in time to see a gook pull his rifle up to shoot at us, so I grabbed my M-16 with one hand and shot him in the head, then announced, "Since I was the one who triggered the ambush I'm dismounting the track to search for bodies."

As I stepped down into the dark and walked hunched over in the eeriness of the night, I stumbled over the body of an enemy soldier. An icy sensation shot through my body. Fear and adrenaline took over. I fired three or four rounds into the gook on the ground and peered at him through the darkness to make sure he was dead.

In that moment something happened that I can't explain. It was as though a destructive force overpowered my whole being. I was out of control, yet a cool sick kind of peace took over my entire being. I slowly slid my bayonet out of its sheath, leaned over that lifeless corpse and cut off his ears, snarling through my clenched teeth. "Come on, God! What are You going to do to me now? Nothing! You're a chicken! You'll kill my friends but You won't kill me! You love to see me suffer, don't You? So I'll tear apart anything You have put together!"

Slipping the ears into my pocket, I continued searching for more wounded or dead Viet Cong. It no longer mattered whether I was in danger of becoming a moving target for the enemy. I came across another body with only half a head left and removed the remaining ear, stuffing it in my pocket with the others. In my rage I walked over to another body I had spotted and saw that the head was gone. Looking up, I noticed the rest of the men on the patrol with me were watching my frenzy. I said, "Well, I can't get his ears! They're gone!"

My command sergeant rasped, "Then gut 'im!" Some of the others chanted, "Gut 'im! Come on, do it! Cut 'im open!"

So I took my knife, stuck it in his side and tried to cut him open. "This thing isn't sharp enough!" I complained.

The sergeant in charge yelled, "Here, use this one. It's sharp enough!" He tossed his knife and it stuck in the ground next to me.

I grasped that knife and thrust it into the side of the corpse ripping him open from his waist to his chest. Standing up I kicked his chest wide open and shouted, "Well, God, what are You going to do to me now? Nothing! You ARE a chicken! You'll kill my friends, but You won't kill me!" I pulled my collection of ears out of my pocket and with my bayonet and the ears in the same hand, raised them into the air. Blood from the freshly cut ears streamed down my arm as I repeated shouts of victory. My fellow soldiers roared cries of approval.

Something changed in me that night. I no longer cared if I lived or died. I was hollow on the inside. Nothing really mattered. My life had no value. In fact, as far as I was concerned, my life was over. I was already dead. From that moment on I vowed I would cut the ears off every man I killed personally and have my picture taken with them. They would be my war trophies.

A contest began in my mind to see who lived and who died. Each time, first place would be awarded to the man who remained alive. My mind had been reduced to the level of a savage.

I had been smoking weed, using opium and drinking alcohol heavily for almost five months. I'd lost over thirty pounds because I wasn't eating or sleeping. My main thought was, *Kill or be killed.*

Without the others knowing, I volunteered for missions that were to have been run by married men. Many times I said to myself, If I am killed, no big loss. What do I have to go home to? I convinced myself that my mother didn't love me, even though I knew she did and I molded my character after the pattern of the man she had thrown in jail time after time and finally divorced. Besides, in my mind I was dead anyway.

I had other recurring thoughts as well. As I got high on marijuana and opium, I continued to read the Bible, twisting three Scriptures to fit my needs. The first one was John 15:13 "Greater love has no man than this: that one lay down his life for his friends." I figured if I lost my life while trying to save someone else's, God would forgive me for all the wrong I'd ever done and allow me into heaven.

The other two Scriptures I distorted, using them to condition my mind for killing. They were, "'Vengeance is mine,' saith Pete Wasko" and "Do unto others before they have a chance to do it to you."

There was one other tactic I used to devalue myself. I knew my mother loved me but it made it easier for me to deal with my actions if I believed that she didn't. When someone is under an extreme amount of stress their mind will justify their warped reasoning. If you tell yourself something long enough you will believe it whether it is true or not. So I told myself over and over my mother doesn't love me.

My cousin Frank Wasko was at the same NDP (night defensive position) while serving with an engineer unit. He learned I was cutting ears off everyone I killed during battle and that I was having my picture taken with my trophies. One night Frank came over to my track and asked, "Pete, could I talk with you privately?"

"Any time, Frank!!"

"Do me a favor. Bring those ears with you." I had been saving them in a container filled with alcohol as a preservative. Before I went out on any mission, I always took the top off the container and stared at the ears, stirring them around to psych myself up to kill some more. Often I repeated my favorite scriptures, "'Vengeance is mine,' saith Pete Wasko" and "Do unto others before they have a chance to do it to you."

Frank and I walked to the front of the track and sat down. He looked me square in the eye and said, "Pete, I don't want to get you upset, but we were raised better than this."

Perplexed I asked, "What do you mean, Frank?"

"Come on, Pete! The ears! What's happened to you? I know you're hurting because all your friends are getting killed, but don't stoop to this, Pete! We were raised better than this. Do me a favor. Throw the ears away."

I looked into his eyes and saw not only his concern, but his love for me. So I threw the ears away and never again committed another savage act of that nature.

Frank Wasko (left) and I (right) with our uncle, Captain Dan Settle (middle) who arranged for us to visit him. Our uncle Captain Settle fired artillery support for our unit as well as many others carrying out operations in his area.

Rage

Within a week I was promoted to acting sergeant and track commander of track one-two. (Instead of saying "track eleven" or "twelve", we said "one-one, "one-two," etc.) My best friend Tom Eaton from New Castle, Illinois, was promoted to acting sergeant of track one-seven where the command sergeant was posted.

When Tom had first come into the field he had been assigned to the track I was on. He was the left gunner and I was the right. I'll never forget our first fire fight together. When the North Vietnamese opened up on us, I was in a position where I couldn't shoot, so my job was to supply everyone with ammunition. As I was "humping ammo" as we called it, I realized Tom wasn't shooting. He stood straight and still, almost as though he was in shock. He stared at me as if to say, "What am I supposed to do?" I pointed in the direction where the enemy fire was coming from and screamed, "Shooooot!"

In robot fashion, he turned, grabbed his M-60 machine gun and opened fire. In his fear Tom had forgotten how to shoot in short burst of fire to prevent burning up the gun barrel, so by the time the little skirmish was over he had burnt up the barrel of the M-60, causing it to fire improperly. Tom never had a problem after that incident.

Later on, after a few weeks of one or two daily firefights with the enemy, I was a wreck. (A firefight is a short conflict with the enemy, like an ambush that lasts from a few minutes to several minutes but seems like forever.) I started to lose control of my mind to the fear of being killed. Every time I saw something move outside of what I thought was the norm, I shot at it, giving our position away. One day when we were not in any apparent danger, I just started shooting and crying at the same time. Tom dragged me away from my machine gun and pulled me to my knees. Slapping me several times to bring me to my senses, he said, "Come on, Pete, you're going to give us away! But we can do this. We're going home together. We're going to make it out of here TOGETHER."

You can see that Tom and I had become very close friends because of our experiences together in the months before our promotions. Shortly after we received our promotions, Tom went to Hawaii on R&R {rest and recuperation} to be with his wife for a week. On Tom's first night in the field, after returning from R&R, He came over to my track around 10 or 11:00 p.m., visibly upset, and said, "I need to talk with you, Pete, in private."

We went out to the front of my track which was broken down at the time. Tears welled up in his eyes. "Pete, I've seen my wife for the last time. I know I'm going to die soon."

I tried to calm him down, but he continued, "Pete, I know you've been volunteering for my missions. I can't allow you to go on missions in my place anymore." I had taken his place on a few ambush patrols prior to our promotions.

"We'll see," I told him. While we were talking, we were informed there was a meeting going on at the command post. An enemy base camp had been located, so a few tracks were needed to go out to secure the area. Tom's track was one that was called. I told him, "You stay and I'll go. You just got back from R&R, so you may be a little rusty."

"No!" he resisted. "I can't allow you to take my place any more." Within the hour, Tom's track hit a land mine and Tom was killed.

When I received word of Tom's death, I cried and cried, asking God, "Why, God, why?" Soon my tears of sorrow turned into tears of rage. I walked out into an open area and looked toward the stars with my fist in the air. "GOD, I'LL GET EVEN

WITH YOU FOR THIS! I was willing to die for my friend, but, no, that wasn't good enough for You! You wanted to see me suffer some more! I'll pay You back, You'll see! YOU'LL PAY FOR THIS ONE!"

Pete, at age eighteen, with an M60 machine gun at base camp prior to being wounded a seond time.

> *The mind is the gateway to the soul and you are the gatekeeper.*

(Photo on left) I was the track commander of this track when we hit a land mine with an estimated 100-120 lbs. of dynamite. They tell me I was blown fifty to sixty feet in the air. I was riding in the cupola which you see in the foreground. I landed on the right front side where the ammunition box is. Photo by Gary Johnson.
(Photo on right) Back at base camp shortly after being released from the field hospital. Both photos were taken the same day.

A Miracle

That outburst against God took place December 17, 1968. Four days later as we were coming in from an ambush patrol, a new guy on my track on his first time out was babbling with excitement. "Boy, do I like being in Nam! All the drugs and women I can handle!"

No matter what was going on, his response was, "This is cool! This is cool!"

I told him, "You'll get over the excitement as soon as you've been in some action and one of your buddies is killed. Then you'll be just like me. You won't trust anyone."

The standing joke was, "When it's your turn to sleep, go ahead and sleep, 'cause Wasko isn't going to sleep anyway. Every fifteen minutes while you're on watch, you're going to see his hand come up over the side of that cupola where the 50 caliber machine gun sticks out and you'll hear him say, 'Are you awake?' DON"T go to sleep!"

Soon it was the new guy's turn to stand guard. After the first fifteen minutes, when I put my hand over the cupola and pulled myself up, he froze.

I called him by his name twice. "Come on, snap out of it! Are you okay?"

"Man!" he said. "I thought you were a gook coming up. I didn't know what to do!"

Our track was the last of the three that came out of the jungle the next morning. As we approached the road, and headed toward our base camp right next to a Vietnamese village, I remember looking at a nearby bush to see if anyone was hiding behind it and wondering how Tom felt when he hit that land mine. *Did he know what happened? Was he in any pain? BOOOM!*

The next thing I knew, I was laying on my left side and Gary Johnson from Moss Point, Mississippi, a man I could trust, was running towards me. Right above my head stood one of my gunners, with most of the muscle and tissue gone from his leg. Helpless, I watched him fall backwards, gasping for air.

Gary kneeled by me and asked, "Are you alright?" I was surprised he asked, because the pain in my legs was so intense that I thought they were both gone.

"My legs," I moaned, "are they still there?"

"Yes," he replied, "but there's a rifle between them, putting pressure on them." He removed the rifle and checked me over. "The only thing I can see wrong is a cut on your chin that's bleeding pretty good. I can't believe you're even alive, Pete. I heard the explosion and turned around to see what was happening and I saw the cupola about fifty feet in the air and you were above it."

Within a few minutes I had my bearings straight, but was madder than a hornet. I rose up and discovered my arm that I had landed on was wounded. Some of the guys from another track discovered wires leading to the land mine which had been command detonated. We believed it was intended for me, since I was always, we'll say, "agitating" the Vietnamese in that area.

The choppers flew us back to the field hospital and I was immediately checked over. After they sewed me up I asked, "Is everything okay?"

"Yeah, you're okay. You're free to go back to your unit."

The cut on my face needed only six or seven stitches, but I don't recall what was done to treat my arm,

I went to my one gunner's cot. He was still fighting for air and I wondered if he was going to make it. He tried to tell me something, but I couldn't hear him. I put my ear near his mouth and heard, "Get my camera. Get my camera." I smiled, thinking, *He's going to be okay!*

I walked over to the next cot to check on my new gunner, not realizing how severe his wounds had been. Holes the size of fifty cent pieces had been blown through his intestines. I walked up just as the medics poured gallons of peroxide on his body. They were waiting for another chopper to arrive and fly him to a different hospital.

"You're going to be okay, buddy." I assured him.

"My leg, my leg! Please, Sarge, straighten it out!" I looked at the medic who nodded his approval. As gently as possible I straightened the one leg.

"No, the other one, the other one!" he told me.

I assured him, "They're both straight. You're going to be okay."

The medic informed us that another chopper was on its way and the wounded would be flown out shortly.

I was sent back to the base camp in Xuan Loc to recuperate. The next morning I was so stiff and sore I didn't want to move. A friend of mine who also had been wounded came over to my army cot and said, "Wasko, you need to take a steam bath and get a massage."

I chuckled for two reasons. "Hey, I don't have the five bucks. Besides, I'm too stiff and sore. I don't want to move!"

He pulled a five dollar bill out of his pocket and dropped it on the floor. "If you can get that five, it's yours. Then I'll go get a jeep and take you for a steam bath and a massage."

A few of the other guys saw me trying to reach the money and gathered around my cot to encourage me. "Come on, move, Wasko. You can do it. Be a real man and get up and get that money!"

Somehow I managed to throw myself on the floor, moaning with every move. When I grabbed the money they all picked me up, carried me out to the jeep and dropped me in the back seat. I think the driver hit every hole in the road, laughing each time we bounced.

Ten days later, New Years Eve, 1968, I was sent back to the field and pulled guard duty the first night. On January 7, 1969, seven days after returning to the field, I turned nineteen. Today, when I think about everything I had experienced in my first eighteen years of life, it's hard to imagine it really happened. However, the tough times didn't end there.

Shortly after my nineteenth birthday, my cousin Frank volunteered for my unit with the stipulation that he would be assigned to my platoon, and he was. He had been in the 919th engineers as a heavy equipment operator. Volunteering for my unit wasn't one of his brightest decisions in life. We were both in G-troop, first platoon, Second Squadron Eleventh Armored Cavalry for almost five months, but were never in one firefight together. To me, that was a miracle.

Not long after my cousin Frank had transferred into my unit, our unit was in a heavy firefight with the enemy. I'd just finished getting checked out in the hospital because of the continuous presence of pain in my back from a land mine that I had hit and was on my way back to the unit when the firefight broke out. They flew me and a few others into a hot LZ (landing zone). By the time I got there, Frank had already been dusted off by a medical helicopter. He had been wounded in the lung.

That was a long painful night for me because I couldn't stop thinking about my cousin Frank. *Why did he volunteer for my unit?* I knew he did it because of me. If he didn't make it, I didn't know what I was going to do.

Within the next few days I was told that Frank was still alive, but bleeding internally. If it didn't stop before too long, they would ship him back to the states. The night before they were to ship him out, the bleeding stopped. After a short recovery time he was back out in the field. However, by the time he arrived, I wasn't there. I'd hit another land mine. February 1969, less than two months from the time I'd hit the first one. This time I wasn't so lucky.

We'd been on a search and destroy mission and had captured two Viet Cong. I was "fortunate" enough to have them on my track. We were transporting them to a designated site where we were to turn them over to headquarters. Before we reached our destination I decided to do a little interrogating on my own and pistol-whipped the one between each question I asked him. He wouldn't answer, so I put the barrel of my forty-five in his mouth, pulled the hammer back. And at that very moment a land mine went off.

I remember seeing a lot of brown dirt while I was in the air. I have no idea how I landed on the APC, but remember pulling myself up on my hands and knees. All I could see were explosions underneath me. (We were carrying a lot of explosives and ammunition.) Tracers from the ammo that we had on the track were firing in the air. I crawled along the top of the deck of the track. When I reached the edge, I looked five feet down to the ground and saw nothing but blood. Somehow I rolled off the burning exploding track and hit the ground.

The next thing I remember was someone grabbing me and dragging me out of danger. They asked, "Anything we can do to make you comfortable? The dust off choppers are on their way."

"How are my men?" I inquired as they were preparing me to be moved to a hospital.

One of them said, "Your driver was blown about twenty feet out of the driver's hatch. When we found him he was choking because some of his teeth had been blown down his throat."

I noticed that Barry, one of my gunners, was not up walking around, so I said, "Barry, are you okay?" He gave me a high sign that he would be all right. The E7 sergeant who had been on our track was in bad shape. The cupola had landed on him; he was busted up pretty bad but he lived.

I had blood running out of both ears and shrapnel imbedded in the right side of my head. My knees were so swollen I was unable to walk. They held a poncho over me to protect me from the blazing sun. After they loaded us on the choppers, I remembered nothing more.

I am standing by my new track. This one only lasted about seven weeks when I hit another land mine. I had just turned nineteen when this picture was taken.

Wonder Boy

Some of my friends called me "Wonder Boy" because they couldn't understand how I'd lived. I guess they had been waiting for the fires and the explosions to die down so they could check through the debris for my body or some of my body parts and I came crawling out of the middle of the mess. After they described the whole scenario to me, I thought, *Wonder why I saw nothing but blood when I looked down over the edge?*

My first recollection after the chopper flight was lying in a hospital back at our base camp in Xuan Loc. I remember some of my guys coming to see me. I couldn't walk yet, but they asked. "Pete, how would you like to go out and have a few beers and smoke a couple of joints?"

I answered, "The nurses won't let me out, but if you'd come to the back door around nine o'clock, I'll be there."

At nine sharp the lights were turned out. I rolled off my bed to the floor and crawled under beds to the back door where the guys were waiting. They lifted me up, threw me in the back seat of the jeep and away we went through the pouring rain. After I was totally smashed, we returned to the hospital. Pulling up to the hospital door, the jeep driver beeped the horn and the others shoved me out of the jeep into a puddle of mud. They sped off so they wouldn't be caught or identified.

I think the nurses must have come to the door and picked me up, cleaned me off, put clean hospital pajamas on me and tucked me in bed. All I know is, the next morning when I came to, I was cleaned up and in bed again.

When I was released to return to the field, I found I wasn't much good. My back and knees were always hurting. I was concerned that I couldn't do my job the way I should because of my physical limitations and didn't want anyone to lose their life because of me, so I went back to base camp. We listened to the radio conversations to see what was going on and every time there were fire fights, as they dusted off the wounded, I drove the jeep back and forth to take them to the hospital. I delivered supplies, worked in the mess hall, doing whatever needed done at the time and, of course, did a lot of partying.

A friend and I broke into the mess hall, but the mess ser-geant caught us. Because of my friends' large size, we ran the sergeant over with ease and escaped.

Not long after that night the same mess sergeant was placed in charge of our unit to fill in for our commanding ser-geant who was on R&R. He ordered me into the field, but I refused to go because the injuries I had received from hitting two land mines would not allow me to function very well. I lost my sergeant stripes for disobeying his orders. He gave those orders because he knew I would never jeopardize someone's life. When the regular commanding officer re-turned, he apologized to me, but said, "There's nothing I can do."

From that time on, I took orders from no one. I couldn't believe that after all I'd been through and all I'd done for my unit, some skinny yellow belly mess hall sergeant was allowed to take my stripes away. I stayed drunk and high until my time was up and I could go home.

July 4, 1969. Only eleven days left before I went home. I had to witness three more of my friends die by the friendly fire of one of the new guys in our unit. Two of them had only around thirty days left before they were supposed to go home. On July 15, 1969, at the age of nineteen, I left Viet Nam and headed home.

III

AM I REALLY HOME?

I believe that only my body and spirit came home from Viet Nam. My mind didn't come home for years. For about forty days I couldn't sleep in a bed. Instead I'd pull the mattress off the bed, put it in a corner of my bedroom in my mother's home and lay on it with my back against the wall so I could watch the door.

One day I fell asleep on the couch in the living room. My mother came in and touched my shoulder to awaken me, and before she knew what was happening, I was standing on my feet with my hands around her throat and trembling with fear. When I became aware of where I was and what I was doing, I warned, "Mom, Mom, never touch me again while I'm sleeping!"

Trauma, according to Webster's dictionary, is *"a disordered psychic or behavioral state resulting from mental or emotional stress or physical injury."* After people have been traumatized, their minds are always on the lookout for anything that might be considered an unsafe environment. This danger may be real or only have the appearance of being real. To the brain it doesn't matter, because it cannot tell the difference.

Since this is not a medical book, I won't give a doctor's detailed explanation of the cascade of chemical reactions which take place during intense trauma. However, so the reader can understand a trauma victim's bizarre behavior, I will cover some of the basic problems that do take place in our amazing bodies.

When under a lot of stress, every aspect of life is affected: mental, physical, chemical, social and spiritual. When that stress is caused by intense fear, isolating and destructive habitual negative thought patterns also develop, first on a conscious level. After a while, these patterns get suppressed to the subconscious level and the person shifts to "automatic pilot" to protect himself at all times. The good news is, these destructive negative thought patterns can be recognized and dealt with. One factor about the traumatized brain is often overlooked by the individual as well as the medical community. The person becomes chemically imbalanced.

In addition to damage from the fears of war, brain functions can also be altered by negative life experiences such as rape, molestation by a friend or loved one, a car accident, or the death of a loved one. Although I base my explanation on what happened to me in Viet Nam, it doesn't matter what the trauma was; when the brain receives the negative input, it responds or reacts from a survival mode. It stores every aspect of the traumatizing negative experience and bases most of its reactions to life on similar states of danger recorded in the memories.

That is what happened to me. In Viet Nam nearly everything I experienced was a life-threatening situation. I became conditioned to living by a continuous survival response from a life and death perspective. The problem was, once I was safe at home, even if a situation wasn't life threatening, my mind would involuntarily consider it to be. As I said before, not only does the mind not know the difference between a truth and a lie, the mind doesn't know if a situation is real or imagined.

An example of this is a flashback. Flashbacks are experienced in the mind as vivid recurrences of a past incident and can be based on good or bad memories. Nearly all of my flashbacks were bad. For example, one night, approximately nineteen years after I was home from Viet Nam, on a dark and warm muggy evening I walked outside on the deck of my home. As I looked out into the woods behind my home, in an instant in my mind I was back in Viet Nam. I saw tracers flying back and forth and heard automatic rifles firing all around me. Because I had not yet gained complete control over my flashbacks, all I could do was stand there and cry in frustration. I didn't know how to shut them off.

Negative flashbacks don't happen to war victims only. They can happen to anyone who has been traumatized. Although experiences may differ for each individual, the effects of past trauma are the same. If the brain is not taught how to control or respond to the "rerun" of the remembered trauma in a positive way, it will most likely respond in a negative survival manner.

Although I was back home in a safe environment, my perceived reality continued to see this world as a hostile life-threatening place. So I responded to everyone and every situation as though it was hostile. Most of my interpretations of current life experiences were based on imagination instead of reality. Therefore, without knowing it, I became THE TRAUMATIZER, alarming everyone and every situation in my path.

Most people who have been traumatized operate by this same destructive pattern. They either destroy themselves or the others around them, and much of the time, hurt their loved ones the most. Their victims then set up mental walls to protect themselves from future circumstances, either real or imagined, and then that victim will traumatize someone else. The cycle goes on and on.

But I have great news. This downward cycle can be stopped, not only in your life, but in the lives of others. I will share more about this in a later chapter, but for now, try to parallel my experiences with your own. Your trauma experiences may not be as bad as mine were, or they may be worse, but the effects are the same and I am writing to assure you there is hope.

This is a picture of a bus that had been blown up and burned.
Obviously the South Vietnamese that were on it did not live. The
two soldiers were in the South Vietnamese Army. The South
Vietnamese lost the most; their loved ones, homes and country.
War affects everyone, even the North Vietnamese lost a lot. In a
war there are no winners.

The Effects of War

I returned from Viet Nam on July 15, 1969, and was discharged from the army in March of 1970, ninety days early to attend college. Once out of active duty, I found a job and enrolled at Youngstown State University, in Youngstown, Ohio, majoring in nursing. However, I had to take other classes so I would have a more rounded education and one I chose was Political Science, not a good choice for a Viet Nam vet in 1970.

I had been back from Nam less than a year and many people were still protesting the war. One day in Political Science Class the professor was talking against the Viet Nam war. What was coming out of his mouth was not settling well with me. I did my best to remain in my chair and control myself by tapping my eraser on the table.

"People are stupid to go to Viet Nam and die for nothing," he commented. That did it! Forcing myself to maintain an appearance of calmness, I stood up, gathered my books and supplies under my arm and walked toward the door, motioning with my finger for the professor to follow me.

Once we were both outside the classroom, I waited until he shut the door, then dropped my books to the floor, grabbed him by the neck and slammed him against the door.

Through clenched teeth I rasped, "I was one of those crazy people who went to Nam and I had a lot of friends get killed and they DIDN'T die for nothing! They died trying to save others including me and your sorry self!"

Releasing him, I picked up my books, walked out of the building, got in my car and headed for the nearest friendly bar.

At the bar, the news was on the TV. I listened to the men sitting near me as they protested the war and thought to myself, *This guy next to me, should I kill him today, or let him live? Well, I think I'll let him live, because killing him isn't worth spending the rest of my life in jail.* It was all I could do to maintain self control.

The next morning at work I was still a mess, shaking all over and unable to focus my mind on my responsibilities. I couldn't do my job properly because all I could think of was what happened at college and the bar the day before.

Lou was the operator of the machine I was working on. A tall black man, he was a bouncer at a bar until he turned his life over to the Lord. Lou often tried to talk to me about the Lord, but I always shook my head "No" and walked away. When Lou noticed I had tears streaming down my face, again he offered the healing love of the Lord, and again I refused.

He told me, "The plant manager is a former alcoholic, but now he's a Christian. Go talk to him. I'm sure he'll understand and give you time off to get some help."

I took Lou's advice and explained to Don the plant manager that I was having problems adjusting from the war. He said, "Take as much time off as you need. When you feel you can handle the job again it will be here for you. Don't worry you WILL always have a job here."

I left work and drove straight home. Walking into the house, I grabbed a beer from the refrigerator and started drinking. My mother came into the room and asked, "Pete, why aren't you at work? You're drinking so early in the morning?"

My poor mother! I unloaded all my frustrations on her. My brother Paul had just gone to bed because he had worked night shift. My screaming woke him up, so he came storming into the kitchen and demanded to know, "What is your problem?"

I smashed my beer onto the counter top, looked him in the

eyes and said, "Paul, I think you'd better get out of here."

For a few long moments of silence Paul continued to glare at me, his out-of-control brother. Then he stared at my mother as if to say, "Mom, I am not leaving you here with Pete until you say it is okay." She nodded her head and, understanding what she meant, Paul left the room. As Mom observed the tears of frustration and emotional pain roll down my face, she asked, "Is it okay if I call the doctor to get something for your nerves? I know how you must be suffering mentally."

"Yes," I said, regretting my outburst and realizing something must be done. So she phoned our doctor and explained the situation.

The doctor called in a prescription and instructed her, "Give him one every eight hours. They'll make him sleep."

Mom woke me up every eight hours without fail and gave me another pill to keep me down. Finally, about three days later, I came to and went out drinking.

The next thing I remembered was a black man and his wife walking out of their house and standing on the street in front of me. I had blood all over me and cuts on my arm. He instructed his wife, "Go back into the house," then asked me, "Can I take you to the hospital?" Later I learned that I had been walking up the street punching out windows.

I retorted, "I don't need any help!"

"Can I give you a ride anywhere?"

"Do you know where the Ohio Street Hotel is?"

"Yes."

In my first conscious memory after that, I was walking out of the hotel with my mother and Uncle Suds behind me. I turned and put my fist through the window right beside my mother's head, ripping my arm open on the jagged edges of the glass. Mom screamed with terror. When I saw the alarmed look in her eyes, I explained, "See, Mom, you don't even know me. You thought I was going to hit you. I'd never hurt you! You're my mother."

Then I heard someone say, "Come on, we've got to get him to the hospital."

Ambrose Gassaway, the man on the left, was killed on July 4, 1969, only eleven days before I came home. Two other men from my unit were killed that night as well, Raymond Pirrman and Jimmy West.

The Mental Institution

I don't remember much about my hospital visit except waking up covered with blood and in a frenzy, fighting to break free from restraints so I could get away. I swore and screamed, "When I get loose, I'll kill every one of you!"

One of the doctors gave me a shot to knock me out, but it didn't do the job. I continued to hallucinate and rave. "Bring my brother Glenn home from Viet Nam. He's going to get killed! I'll go back over, but bring Glenn home! We've got to get Glenn home!"

The doctor asked for my mother's permission to give me another shot so he could clean me up and sew up the cuts and she gave her consent. They waited and waited, but I continued to rage and thrash as much as the restraints would allow. So the doctor told my mother, "I'm going to have to give him another injection. It could kill him, because I don't know what drugs or how much alcohol he has inside of him. I need a consent form signed in order to give him a third shot."

Later on my mother recalled, "I remember hearing your screaming cries from the horror you'd been through and realized that mentally you were living in hell. I decided that what you were reliving had to be dealt with somehow, so I signed the papers permitting the doctor to give you another shot."

That third one knocked me out. They checked my vitals regularly as they stitched the deep cuts in my arm. After the final check, the doctor announced, "He's going to make it, but he's going to sleep for two or three days."

A half an hour later I came to and with violence began to flail, pushing the strength of my restraints to the limit. They decided to transfer me to another local hospital which had a psych unit, but they refused to take me in my condition. So I was taken by ambulance to a government mental institution named Leechfarm in Pittsburgh, Pa.

By the time we reached Leechfarm – What a name for a hospital! – I was calm enough to be transported in a wheelchair. Once we were in the lobby, I stood and walked to the admitting desk and signed myself in.

"I have to go to the bathroom," I told the nurse, planning to climb out of the window and escape. But to my surprise, two big guards dressed in white accompanied me. This ruined my escape.

The next thing I remembered was waking up in my room in 44 West, bound in a straight jacket. Soon two aids unlocked my door and came in. They took the straight jacket off and escorted me to a room where they sat me in a chair in front of a doctor seated behind a desk. He said, "Pete, my name is Dr B." Then he asked, "Do you know where you are?"

I stared into his eyes for a moment and then looked around at the people dressed in hospital clothes. I replied, "I'm in a hospital somewhere."

"Well," he said with a kind smile, "it's sort of a hospital. Pete, you're in a nut house!"

I shot out of the chair and over the desk and wrapped my hands tightly around his neck. Both of us fell over the back of his chair. I could hear a lot of screaming and felt my pants come down and a sharp stab in my butt.

I have no idea how long I was unconscious. The next thing I was aware of was two men dressed in white coming into my room and escorting me back to the same doctor. All the same people sat around me. I was guided to the chair in front of the desk and, once again, I didn't take my eyes off the doctor. Finally he said, "Pete, I would like to take that straight jacket off, but first I would like to explain the purpose of our first meeting. We tell everyone on their first visit to this office that they are in a nut house. If they don't react there isn't much hope for them. But, Pete, there's a lot of hope for you. Now, may we remove the straight jacket without you getting violent?" I nodded my consent.

Life at Leechfarm remains vivid in my memories. At the building called 44 West I would get on an elevator and go to the fourth floor. If I stepped off the elevator and turned left, I came to an intersecting hallway. If I turned right and looked down the corridor, I would see two rooms on the right and two on the left. At the end of the hallway were double doors with a treatment room on the other side where shock treatments were given. I remember every step of the way.

My private quarter was the first room on the left, one door away from the shock therapy room. There was a dresser and a bed and one window decorated with wire, woven and encased in blown glass making a beautiful diamond pattern.

I can remember how I would leave my room, turn right, go to the first hallway and turn right again and pass the nurses' station on the left where they dispensed our "ever-calm" vitamins when needed. My vitamin by my doctor's choice was the drug Thorazine. On down the corridor was the entertainment room, a large room with desks for playing card games, building puzzles, etc. I was not interested in games. Instead, I would stand in the corner, away from everyone and watch World War II vets, Korean vets and many others pass their time.

Everyone was there from different causes, but for the same reason. Something was wrong with the way our brains processed information from the outside world. We functioned at a more "visionary" level than most people; a hallucinating state, but a "higher level of thought" from the mental patient's point of view. For example, one man had visions of Jesus coming in a white limousine to take him out of the "fine hotel" in which we were staying. Another man decided to "borrow" a commercial airliner while all the passengers were still aboard. Another individual, a foot doctor from World War II, smoked cigarettes through his ears. One man about my age was "hiding from the secret service." While at home one weekend for a short visit, he'd run his head into a door while trying to get away from the imaginary secret police and was paralyzed from the neck down. The saddest case was a man who waited for someone to throw a cigarette butt into the urinal. He'd fish it out, dry it out and smoke it. As I explained earlier, a "higher" level of thought.

Our personal guards, dressed in white, allowed all this to continue. Everywhere I went, I was accompanied by aides. I chose to look at them as my body guards rather than those who protected others from me.

One day during my relaxation time at this fine resort, I was escorted out of my plush quarters and taken to a room where I was given some Thorazine before a psychiatrist tried to outwit me with the familiar ink spot test. He instructed, "Look at these spots, Pete, and tell me what you see."

The pattern on one of the cards made no sense to me. "I can't come up with anything for that one," I told him.

"Come on," he pushed, half jeering. "It's obvious. Don't you see a naked man and woman making love?"

"You're a pervert!" I retorted, cussing at him. "YOU need help!" But he was the one giving the test, not me.

About two weeks after I was admitted to Leechfarm, as I stood in line to receive my Thorazine, I decided to trick the nurse who was dispensing the meds. I tipped the Dixie cup containing a little red pill to my lips, tossed the pill into my mouth and hid it between my teeth and gums. When she checked my mouth she couldn't see it, so I was able to go into the bathroom and spit the medication down the toilet.

About three days later, one of my inmates who knew what I was pulling, advised me, "You need to act tired and drowsy, Pete, or they'll know you haven't been taking your meds." So I did as he suggested.

One Friday a man dressed in white came into my room, sat with me on the side of my bed and said, "I've read your entire chart and know what a rough time you've had. But I believe if you can get out of here, you'll be okay. If you don't get out of here this weekend it'll be too late. On Monday they plan to give you shock therapy which will damage your brain forever. I've arranged for you to have a pass to walk around the grounds because of your good behavior. I recommend that once you get outside you run and never come back."

Well, he didn't have to tell me twice! He arranged for the pass while I phoned my cousin Frank and insisted that he come and visit me. Since he was using my car I didn't give him an option. When he arrived and we walked outside, I said, "I want to show you around the campus, Frank. Give me the keys to my car and I'll drive you around."

"Promise you won't leave hospital grounds?"

"Trust me." After a brief hesitation he gave me the keys.

I slid into the driver's seat and began to drive him around. But when we got near the exit I sped out. Frank panicked! "They'll put me in jail for helping you escape!"

Ignoring him I asked, "Which way do we go?"

He wouldn't tell me, so I switched on the left turn signal. Frank said, "No! Turn right." Home we went.

Once we were home, I assured Frank I would call the hospital and tell them I was not coming back. That I did.

I was uneasy for days, thinking they were going to send someone after me. Hearing nothing for ninety days, I went back to the VA Hospital as an outpatient for counseling. My counselor never detected that I was coming to my session higher than a kite on drugs. After about eleven months he released me.

My cousin, Frank Wasko, left, and my brother, Glenn, both Viet Nam vets and deceased. Neither would talk about Viet Nam and both died in their forties from heart disease. Frank was also a victim of Agent Orange.

The Adrenaline Rush

I believe a vet or anyone who has been in life-threatening situations, real or imagined, becomes addicted to the adrenaline rushes they experience while they're in a combat zone or a crisis situation. When vets get back to the states, or when others return to normal surroundings, they can't handle it, so they create a hyper-awareness environment in order to recreate the adrenaline rush they've become accustomed to feeling.

One beautiful night in October, 1971, I was at my uncle's bar, the Ohio Street Hotel, drinking COLT 45 malt liquor and taking codeine pain killers. Needless to say, I was feeling pretty good. So after I left the bar and drove away. I ran the stop sign as I turned to the left. Then I veered to the right, but failed to negotiate a sharp curve. By this time my vehicle was on the wrong side of the road and I was looking into the headlights of an oncoming car. Unfortunately that vehicle happened to be a police car. He had to swerve off the road in order to miss me. That started "The Chase"!

The cop made a big U turn to come after me, but the steel mill had just changed shifts, so he had traffic, stop signs and red lights to contend with. I didn't. I sped through them all without stopping, driving between homes, running over bushes and through stop signs. In moments five police cars were chasing after me. I was excited! This was like being in the movies!

I KNEW I could get away! The adrenaline was definitely pumping. I remember shutting off my head lights so they wouldn't be able to see me as I sped over sidewalks, through peoples' yards and down alley ways. In my mind, I believed I'd done a great job of escaping. Since I couldn't see my pursuers I believed they couldn't see me either. As you can see I had ascended into that higher level of thought again

I lost them! I concluded. *I'm free!* Laughing, I stopped the car in front of my aunt's home, got out, and found myself looking down the barrel of a pistol. The policeman behind the gun shouted, "Put your hands up and turn around!" I complied.

"Put your hands on the roof of the car!" he ordered. I did.

By that time my Aunt Virginia and Uncle Suds had come out of their house and joined all their half-awake but curious neighbors. Police cars with flashing lights, spotlights and armed policemen surrounded me. One officer frisked me, while another kept his gun aimed toward me. After I'd been completely searched and I turned around, my aunt stepped between the aimed gun and myself. She screamed at the officer, "Put that gun away! He's NOT a criminal!"

As the policeman holstered his pistol, my fist plowed underneath his jaw and picked him up a couple of feet off the ground. Seven cops moved in and beat the living daylights out of me. I was bruised and sore for a month.

Twenty one charges were filed against me that night, including assault and battery against a police officer. But because my brother Paul knew the mayor, I walked away with a thirty five dollar ticket for not yielding to the right of way. I realize today that this was not luck, but God. He had a plan for my life and a jail sentence was not included in His plan.

I believe God used my brother Paul to protect me. He was always there for me when I needed him. Without fail he would find a way to get me out of trouble. One night I phoned him when I knew I was too drunk to drive. Since it was about three in the morning he was home in bed sleeping. But he got out of bed and drove about fourteen miles in one direction to pick me up and take me home. However, when he arrived at the scene of my distress, I had developed a second wind of energy and was waiting there for him with two young ladies, one for my great brother Paul and one for me. Without speaking a word he grabbed me, pulled me out of the tavern, threw me into his car and drove me home.

My adrenaline rushes could not be compared with the intensity of those I'd experienced in Nam every time someone tried to kill me. Why do people do such bizarre things? These rushes, needed to mask extreme residual feelings of fear and terror, become addictive and are the reason a lot of vets and others create high-tense stress situations.

Similar feelings affect police officers when they are in life-threatening circumstances, or firefighters while fighting a raging fire. Other examples would be paramedics, nurses or doctors trying to save a life in an emergency situation. There are a lot of victims of domestic violence and rape who experience the same feelings. The problem is always, how do you shut off the adrenaline?

An adrenaline high is difficult to explain, but I'll try. Excess adrenaline pumping through your arteries is like nothing you've ever experienced. Every cell in your body comes alive, on the alert, like never before. It feels like every hair on your body is standing straight up, with eyeballs on each hair that are looking for the threatening danger which lurks within your presence. Muscles tense, developing a supernatural surge of strength causing you to be capable of performing phenomenal inhuman feats. Vision becomes crystal clear, enabling you to see the peach-like fuzz on a bug swaying with the slightest movement of air. Reactive movement is timely and accurate with precision similar to that of a highly sophisticated radar tracking system. The mind is so active and alert it can keep the body in this highly aggressive state as long as needed without tiring. You feel you could defeat the world single-handed, so why would you want to shut off the adrenaline?

Most people prefer the rush to facing and dealing with the hidden underlying intense fear, therefore the mind involuntarily creates situations, remembered or imagined. That is exactly what I did over and over again. I created life-threatening circumstances in my mind and then lived them out. Unfortunately they involved and affected the people I loved and cared about the most – my wife, my children, my family. You will see as my story continues.

> *Your life is entangled with*
> *the words of your mouth.*

Sick Revenge

Shortly after the chase I began to date a young lady. One day, after I talked with her from my vehicle which I'd parked in her parents' driveway, I put my car in reverse. Forgetting to look behind me, I backed into her sister's boyfriend's car. I knew him and his family; they lived close to my parents. His brother and I had gone to high school together.

I contacted his mother and explained that I already had several driving problems on my record. So I asked her to take the damaged car, find out what it would cost to repair, and I would pay for the expense. "Please don't turn it in to your insurance company," I pleaded. "I'm already in the high risk category and this will increase my rates even more."

She agreed, got the estimates brought them to me and I paid her so she could get their car fixed. After receiving the money from me, she turned the incident in to her insurance company. Since I had no proof that I had already paid her in cash for the damages, she got paid twice and my insurance premiums went up.

I kicked into my old mental mode: "VENGEANCE IS MINE, SAITH PETE WASKO" and blew up her mail box several times. The ultimate revenge took place when I caught her alone in the grocery store just as she was about finished with her shopping. Her grocery cart was completely full.

The ol' adrenaline kicked in as opportunity loomed before me. I was elated! She was the enemy and she was MINE!

Wearing my sleeveless blue jean jacket, with my long hair flowing, I approached her slowly with an evil glint in my eyes and a taunting grin on my face. A look of terror froze on her face. I stopped in front of her and stared into her eyes, nodding my head up and down. With an evil terrifying chuckle, I stated, "You're mine now. Oh yeah, I've got you now, don't I?"

I circled her as she clung to her grocery cart. "You're all mine and no one can help you. I've been waiting for this moment and today I am going to get even with you for the wrong you did to me."

Laughing and taunting, I encircled her grocery cart a couple more times. All of a sudden she panicked and took off running for her car, leaving her groceries in the store. I'd won the standoff! She was terrified and thought she was escaping from a life-threatening situation when all I wanted to do was scare her. The adrenaline rush was hardly worth the effort, but the feeling of payback was sweet at the time.

*You will never move beyond
your confession.*

Drug Abuse

By this time I had decided to move into the Ohio Street Hotel, which consisted of twelve or so boarding rooms where mostly alcoholics lived above my uncle's Ohio Street Bar. My abode was room #1, the first room on the right hand side at the top of the steps. Six feet wide and ten feet long, the room was a dingy grey with no curtains, just a blind on the window. It was furnished with an army cot and a dresser. I made sure a bottle of whiskey was always present on top of the dresser. My uncle charged me a dollar a day to live there but would never accept the rent payment.

I entertained a continuous line of drunken guests in his bar. We were always shooting pool, drinking and drawing a lot of attention to ourselves. I loved putting on a show for everybody who came in. When I got drunk, I became wild and crazy, but remained a pretty good pool player, known for my "I don't care" attitude. Hey, I was free!

I believe most people are brought up with a set of values and a moral conduct by which they were to live. These values become an ingrained part of their belief system. One way to change a person's belief system is by inserting doubt into their current belief system. Another way beliefs and codes of conduct can be changed is by causing a person to lose respect for themselves. They will, in turn, lose respect for others. The use of drugs and alcohol will help tear down those value systems by destroying a person's self esteem. Because of all the bad decisions I had made against the values and morals that I was raised with, plus the excessive use of drugs and alcohol, I had lost all self respect as well as all respect for others.

I only did acid a few – okay, maybe a dozen – times. That's only a few, right? But every time I took this drug, all I could talk about was becoming a preacher. I preached sermons of condemnation and damned everyone to hell. Then I'd switch and preach eternal life and forgiveness. My friends laughed hysterically as I entertained them with my drug-induced preaching. What a contradiction of values and lifestyle!

I was always high on painkillers, speed, marijuana and alcohol. This combination brought the best adrenaline rushes. It wasn't that the drugs were so much fun, but doing them without getting caught was. One method I managed to get away with was through taking advantage of two doctors to obtain diet pills.

I was six feet tall and weighed in at 165 pounds. One doctor would weigh me, take my blood pressure and ask me what I wanted.

"Doc, I've gained five pounds," I would explain with all the false sincerity I could muster up. "I don't want to be overweight and need something to kill my appetite. How about writing me out a prescription for diet pills?"

Without a problem I'd have a prescription for a thirty day supply in my hand. I'd thank the doctor, wave goodbye and say, "See you in a month!"

From there I'd go to the second doctor and do the same thing. Also I was getting T4s (Tylenol with codeine) from the VA hospital to help control the pain from the wounds I'd received during the war. So everything I did, I did high or drunk. A lot of the time I had a case of wine stashed in the trunk of my car and a bag of drugs in the glove box.

In addition to taking delight in my own highs, I received a lot of personal enjoyment from getting other people high. Most of the time after my initial invitation they responded by feeling paranoid. This was my time to move in and attack their minds, not to mention tearing down their value system. Mine had been destroyed already, so why not theirs?

"Hey, I'm Satan's right hand man!" I bragged. I knew I was going to burn in hell and wanted as many people as I could snag to burn there with me. Misery loves company! The thought planted in my subconscious mind was, *Whatever God puts together, I will tear apart.* Remember, while I was in Viet Nam I made a vow that I would get even with God for killing my friends!

Talk about losing self respect! On several different occasions, I took syringes, injected myself with speed, and then drew my blood back out the same hole into the needle. I used the loaded needle as a pen to write my initials, "PJW," on the front of the shirt I was wearing.

I'd put away a case of beer a day, without feeling much of the effect because I was using so much speed. After a while I switched from beer to drinking a gallon of wine a day. I'd wake up at five a.m., smoke a joint and drink a quart of wine. Then I'd go back to bed and sleep until I had just enough time to get to work at seven. During the thirty minute drive to work, I'd consume another quart of wine. On my thirty minute lunch break I'd drink another quart, plus a six-pack of beer. That would hold me until I got off work. Then I'd drink another quart of wine on my way home. I rarely displayed the affects of the alcohol – it was just something to get rid of the pain.

On one occasion while I was working overtime, my boss caught me drinking out of a wine bottle and said, "You know I'm going to have to write you up for this?"

I grabbed him and slammed him up against the wall and held him there as I poured wine down his throat. Then, splashing wine all over his face and head, I proclaimed, "If I go down, you're coming with me! And I'll bet the price you pay will be a lot higher than mine!" He didn't turn me in and I believe it was not because of the threat, but because he feared what I might do to him in retaliation.

I don't remember much of what happened during one particular three-year period. People have helped me piece my life together. I lived with a blonde named Linda who I'd met when I was in the hospital in traction for back pain. One day after I'd been bowling with my friends, I went home high on drugs. Without saying a word, I went upstairs to our bedroom and threw all my clothes in a bushel basket.

"What are you doing?" Linda cried out, nearly hysterical.

"I'm leaving!"

"But I love you! I thought we were going to get married."

I think I was in love, too, but I was scared. I didn't understand all the thoughts and emotions swirling around in my head, so I switched into my "I don't care" mode and told her, "Hey, I came in a basket and I'm leaving in a basket."

That was in 1971. From that point until 1974 I don't remember very much. Some of what I know has been told to me by others.

In February, 1974, I went to the Ohio Street Hotel to shoot pool with my brother Glenn, drinking, smoking marijuana and taking speed as usual. I had already been in a fight in another bar and had blood all over me.

When Glenn noticed my appearance and my condition, he said, "Man, you've got to get some help. Viet Nam really messed you up!"

I retorted, "You're a Nam vet and you're messed up, too!"

We began to argue. I grabbed my brother, threw him up against a freezer in the back room of the bar and pulled a switch blade out of my pocket. He'd brought that knife to me from Germany as a gift. Before he could react, I had the blade at his neck and yelled, "I'll cut your throat wide open! I'll kill you in a heart beat!"

Glenn never backed down. "Go ahead, do it!" he screamed back at me just as loudly as I was screaming at him.

My Aunt Inez ran to the scene of the fight. "Don't kill him, Pete! Don't kill him! Pete, he's your brother. Don't kill him!"

Something had happened to me while I was in that bar. Something had tripped in my brain which put me in a trance-like state. I didn't know who I was or where I was. I do remember hearing others yelling at me to stop and also my mother showing up and trying to calm me. "He's your brother,

Pete. Don't kill him."

The pleading tone of her familiar voice penetrated the callousness of my heart. I put the knife away and let him go. I went up to my room, threw all my clothes into a bag and headed for my car. I was off to Florida!

About a half mile away from my uncle's bar there is a bridge that spans the Allegheny River. Part way across the bridge my senses began to return. *How could I have done that? I love my brother!* I stopped my 1973 Volkswagen Super beetle, removed the knife from my pocket and held it in my hand, thinking, *This is a gift my brother bought for me and I was going to use it to kill him!* Without hesitation I threw the knife into the river.

The next thing I remember, I was driving through Columbus, Ohio, more than three hours away from home. I stopped and phoned someone, but I don't remember who, and said, "I'm in Columbus, Ohio, and I'm going to Florida. I don't know when I'll be back."

I stayed in Florida for two weeks, then came back home. The strange thing was, I didn't drink much or do drugs there like I did at home.

Take reponsibility for your life because it is what you have made it to be now and it will be what you make it to be in the future.

PRINCIPLES OF THOUGHT

- *Your thoughts expand*

- *Your thoughts create whatever you believe to be true*

- *Your thoughts are eternal and continue to produce results until they are stopped or rethought.*

IV

MARRIAGE FOR THE WRONG REASON

Marriage is something God intended to be a beautiful growing relationship of love and respect between a man and a woman, something that is supposed to happen only once in a lifetime. When most people get married, they don't realize the depth of the commitment involved or that marriage is forever, "until death do us part." When that "forever" is shattered, many people are affected; the adverse effects do not involve just two people. Divorce creates a ripple affect, hurting all the people connected with their lives.

A wounded damaged person who is not capable of handling the responsibility of marriage is like a person standing in the middle of a pond with ripples going out in all directions. He or she is facing only in one direction and can see only the people in front of them. But there are also people out to the side and to the back who are affected by the ripples. Divorce affects all the people they know and love. Once you and I realize how much the poor decisions we make can hurt other people, we will desire to change our behavior so we can help others instead of blaming and hurting them.

In other words, if you are in a bad marriage, work on you.

Don't work on your spouse. If you have a bad relationship with your boss, work on yourself first. If you have a bad relationship with God, He is not the problem. You are the problem. If you have difficulty with your pastor or your neighbor, work on you first. Go to God and ask Him to help you see what's going on inside you. What does He want you to do? What is He trying to get you to see about yourself? Learn to look at your situations through God's eyes instead of your own. I hurt a lot of people before I learned this.

Soon after I got home from Florida at the end of February, I made arrangements to pick up a young woman I had been dating off and on for awhile and take her to my mother's home for a family dinner. While we were eating and chatting, she announced to my family, "Did you know Pete and I are getting married in August?"

I was shocked! So shocked I can't remember how my family reacted. But I decided, *Hey, why not play along?* After we left my mother's house, I asked her, "What brought that announcement on? We aren't even engaged."

Her response was, "Oh, I guess I'll try anything once."

I thought, *Well, why not? I'll try anything once, too!* We set a date.

My mind was never focused on wedding plans. That was her responsibility. I was too involved with my own agenda, partying and sowing my wild oats as much as I could before getting tied down. I believed I had to get all that out of my system and time was running out.

For the next five months, while she was busy planning, I "dated" as many women as I could and continued overindulging in drugs and alcohol. One night, about two weeks before the big day, I invited a lady to spend the night with me in my apartment where my bride-to-be was going to move after our wedding.

My fiancée called the apartment again and again throughout the night, but I wouldn't answer the phone. About three a.m. the phone rang once more. In disgust I answered it, only to hear my fiancée shout, "WHO IS THERE WITH YOU?"

"No one," I replied, trying to hide my irritation over the interruption.

She yelled, "You know, you keep acting like this and I'll call off our wedding!"

I replied, "Hey, you do what you've gotta do!" and hung up.

You must remember I "died" a long time ago back in Viet Nam. My emotions were inoperative. The things that thrilled or upset others didn't faze me a bit, because when a person chooses to "die" in order to exist, all compassion and empathy become frozen.

Jesus said, "I am the resurrection and the life. He who believes in me, though he may die, he shall live."

I am standing to the far right. The cross on my gun shield was made from masking tape. I would get high smoking marijuana and read the Bible because I wanted to know more about God and I wanted to get even with Him. I blamed Him for allowing so many of my friends to be killed.

Honeymoon

I began the day of my wedding at the apartment drinking Mad Dog 20/20 wine and smoking marijuana. I don't remember if anyone was there with me or not. All I remember was, time was running out. When I arrived at the church, the music was playing and everyone was waiting for my arrival. Standing on the steps at the back of the church, I debated, *Should I ... or shouldn't I?* Finally I was drunk enough and high enough, I answered my own question out loud. "I'll try anything once."

I remember nothing about the wedding or the reception, unless you count the fact that I had innumerable shots of whisky and repeated to myself many times, "What have I done?"

My bride and I had planned to spend our first night together as man and wife at a hotel in Pittsburgh, Pennsylvania, I think! But instead I drove through Pittsburgh and two hours farther to Breezewood, Pennsylvania. She fell asleep, but during the drive she would occasionally lift her head up, look around and say, "Come on, Pete. Pull off and get a hotel room."

When we finally stopped at a hotel and checked in, she crawled into bed and I slumped into a chair, turned the lights off and fell asleep. About an hour and a half later I awoke and groped my way over to the bed.

"Wake up," I told my new bride as I shook her. "Come on. This is it. We've got to get to Virginia Beach."

That's about all I remember about our honeymoon. I can't

tell you if we were gone one week or two. I had taken about a hundred hits of speed and a couple ounces of marijuana with me. I indulged in the drugs as often as I could, without her awareness I think!

My brother, Paul Wasko (right) and me. My brother, Paul, is also my best friend. It was also because of him I was spared from myself and trouble with the law.

My Firstborn

Long before the first couple of months were over, "wedded bliss" had vanished and the phrase "The honeymoon is over" had become the theme of my mental attitude. I was already involved in an affair with a married woman who was on the outs with her husband. About three months into the affair I learned that this woman had become pregnant with my first child. When she found out she was pregnant, she decided the best thing she could do, keeping her family's best interest in mind, was to end our affair.

In August, 1975, I learned that my first born child, a daughter, had arrived in the world, but I wasn't allowed to see her because of the situation. On March 1, 1976, my wife gave birth to my first son, Peter J. Wasko, Jr.

A few months later, while at a picnic, my son and my daughter sat side by side. My head swam with decisions about how to handle the situation. I looked at my son. I was so proud of him! *Should I let my wife know this girl is my daughter? If I tell my wife, I know she'll leave me. Then my son will be raised without me.* I looked at my daughter and longed to be able to raise her as my own. If I let anyone know that this little girl belonged to me, there was still no certainty that I would be permitted to have a part in her life. In fact, if I did that, there was no certainty that I would be able to be a visible father to either of my children! So I endured the rest of the picnic while trying to deal with the miserable situation I had created for myself.

My cousin, Frank, and me two months after I received my third Purple Heart for being wounded in action. My cousin had already been wounded two times and received his third Purple Heart shortly after this photo was taken.

You're Out of Here

The vow to get even with God I'd made in Nam remained alive in my mind. Nearly every action I took, every decision I made was tainted with my promise to get even with Him. I was driven to destroy anyone or anything God held dear.

Even as a newly married man, I dated both single and married women just to spite HIM. My anger toward God was so deep and dark that it drove me to destroy my marriage.

About a week after my son was born I informed my wife that I wouldn't be coming home that night because I was going to tend bar at a private overnight party. In reality, I was going on a gambling trip to the Bahamas with the guys.

The next day, during the time some of our friends had come to our apartment, she found out that I hadn't been bar tending and demanded to know where I'd been. I was lying on the bed too hung over from the night before to visit with our friends. She stayed on my case until I finally laughed and said "Okay, okay! I'll tell you! I went to the Bahamas with the guys."

Never knowing whether or not to trust my word, she retorted, "I don't believe you!"

So I reached in my pocket and pulled out stirrers with "Bahamas" printed on them. "Here," I told her, "I brought you some souvenirs."

For my wife that was the last straw. She ran into our bedroom and began to throw all of my clothes and belongings outside the bedroom door. "Get out!" she screamed. "And don't ever come back!" Laughing, I scooped up my belongings. I looked at our friends, grinned, shrugged my shoulders and said "I guess I'm out of here." I left, unable to sense her pain or her anger.

When I arrived at my mother's home, mom looked at her son nearly hidden behind a pile of clothes and other belongings and asked, "Pete, what's wrong?"

"We're having a few problems," I explained. "Could I stay here for a few days?"

After I sobered up I called my wife and explained to her, "There were no women there last night. Let's try to make it for our son's sake. We need to try and make this marriage work." She agreed!

During this time I was working as a bar tender in a place called the R&R Lounge where I had become involved with a woman who was a regular there. A few nights after moving back with my wife and son I quit work early and took this woman with me to another bar. We hadn't been there long, when the bar tender came to me and said, "Pete, you have a phone call."

I took the phone. It was my wife. "Pete, what's going on?"

"I'm having a few drinks with the guys," I lied.

"Pete, I want to meet you there. Let's have a couple of drinks and talk."

"No! Don't bother to come here."

She persisted. "I'm coming anyway. I don't care what you say."

I finished my drink and told the woman who was with me, "We've gotta leave."

The moment my companion and I walked out of the bar, we found ourselves facing my wife. She had called me from the payphone outside the bar. I'd been caught!

After an extremely heated conversation, I took my girlfriend home and, undisturbed by the whole incident, went back to my mother's home once again, asking if I could stay awhile until I got things straightened out.

Mental Hardness

Two days later, March 23, 1976, only three weeks after my son was born, while at work I received a phone call from my dad's live-in girlfriend. "Pete, your father's had a heart attack and I think he is dead." A co-worker offered to finish my shift, but before I left I called my brother Paul. "Dad's had a heart attack," I told him. "The ambulance is already on its way to his place, so I'm heading there, too."

I arrived at his home just in time to see my father carried down the steps on a stretcher. As he passed by me, my first instinct was to grab hold of his foot. It was cold and rigid. What a familiar feeling! All my friends who had been killed in the war had felt that same way. *Dad didn't make it*, I told myself.

Someone contacted my other brother Glenn who was living in Germany and we waited five days for him to be flown home before we had the funeral. When my wife heard about Dad's death, she phoned and said, "Pete, I know this is going to be hard for you. Why don't you move back home and we'll give it another try? One thing, though. You'll have to quit your job at the bar and leave your girlfriend."

"I'll try it," I said. And I did.

The day before my dad's interment my two brothers and I sat down together to talk about the funeral and about our relationship with our father. I suggested, "Let's all wear white suits to his funeral. This way we can make a statement. His life on earth was hell but now he's in a better place."

My brothers refused to go along with my idea, so I chose to compromise and wear a powder blue leisure suit. I vowed I would not shed one tear at the funeral. If there was one thing my father had taught me, it was that I must be strong in all circumstances. I was determined to show him how strong I had become.

"I want to be there when they dump the dirt on the old man," I told my brothers. He never taught us much of anything but I remember him repeating to me when I was a little boy, "You've got to be tough, Pete. You've GOT to be tough."

No, I will NOT shed one tear! I'll show him how tough I am!

After the funeral was over I told my brothers I was staying at the cemetery to watch them fill in the grave. Each of my brothers took hold of one of my arms and my brother Paul pleaded, "Pete just get in the car and, please, don't cause any problems."

Upon our arrival at my Brother Paul's house, I jumped in my car and sped back to the cemetery. With my vow in mind, I watched as my father's coffin was lowered into the ground. Just as the first shovel of dirt fell on his casket, I flipped a rose into his grave and declared, "Here's how tough I am, old man!"

Following the family gathering after the funeral, I returned to our apartment and resumed my life of taking drugs and drinking.

V

DELIVERED FROM HELL

I continued to live with my wife, but since I had no job, I stayed home and took care of our infant son. There was never a time that I was sober. I kept on taking drugs and drinking heavily, so heavily that I don't remember where I was or what I was doing. I am told that much of the time I either just sat and stared into space or waxed my Harley, unable to respond to anyone or anything. Finally my wife called my mother and told her that she needed to come and try to get through to me or I would have to be sent back to the mental institution.

Mom came to the apartment and looked into the garage where I was staying with my motorcycle. I told her, "Mom, just stop right where you are. I think you better leave".

My mother wouldn't give up. She retorted. "Pete, your problem isn't with drugs or alcohol. Your problem is with God."

"It's best that you leave, Mom," I warned her again. For me, referring to God was comparable to lighting a match near a gas tank. I was unable to think straight, and every time I looked at her, it was as though I was looking at her through two flaming tunnels.

"I'm not leaving, Pete, until you agree to talk with a minister." She was adamant.

All of a sudden a light bulb came on in my head. I had promised God that I was going to get back at Him for killing all my friends in Viet Nam. My mother's insistence that I see a minister could become the high point of my plan. I thought, *What better way to get back at God for killing my friends than to kill one of His chosen servants?* I looked at Mom and smiled. "Call a pastor and set up a meeting," I told her. The adrenaline began to rise.

"Will you sit down and talk with Pastor Jim Erb?" she asked.

"Sure!" I didn't care who the minister was as long as he was chosen by God. My appointment with Pastor Erb was set up for the next evening at eight o'clock. I was so excited! Now I could get even with God!

I spent all that next day planning every detail of our meeting. I imagined my picture on the front page of the local newspaper under the headline, "Viet Nam Vet Beats Minister to Death with Fist." I planned to show up at his house at eight thirty instead of eight o'clock, so when he opened the door, he would say, "You must be Pete Wasko. You're late." The word "late" was to be my queue to start beating him to death with my fist.

Earlier in the day I ironed my dark blue dress pants and a bright yellow shirt. I looked good in yellow! Besides, I needed to wear something that would be obvious when the news reporters snapped my picture for the front page. To prepare for my big moment, I sat in our apartment all day long, doing drugs and playing over and over in my mind the way it would be when the pastor opened his door. By late afternoon, this was no longer a mental plan, but a reflex.

Just before time to go, I called the girl I was seeing and told her, "I want to see you. Can I stop by for a minute?"

When I arrived, I said, "I can't stay long. I just want you to make sure you buy a newspaper tomorrow and look at the front page. Finally, I'm going to get my revenge against God."

She said "What do you mean 'Get even with God'? What are you talking about?"

"Just get the paper and you'll see! I'll be on the front page!" Then I left.

On my way to Pastor Erb's home I drank a pint of Vodka in less than ten minutes for an extra buzz. I figured, *He won't be able to smell the Vodka on my breath.* I deliberately arrived in front of his home at twenty-five minutes after eight and sat in my car for another five minutes before embarking into what was to be the highlight of my life.

As I got out of the car and walked up the sidewalk towards his house, my fists were clenched and ready for action. It was as though I was walking in a long black hallway with nothing around me but darkness. I could feel my pulse beating in my neck. My heart was ready to pound its way out of my chest. When I finally stopped in front of his door, I just stood there, staring at it. Finally, I slowly dropped my eyes to look at my watch. Exactly eight thirty! I raised my hand and knocked on the door with an unnerving calmness, ready to eliminate one of God's chosen. "Vengeance is mine, saith Pete Wasko" were the words that soothed my mind.

In the moments before he answered the door, I prepared my fist for the first blow. The door opened to expose a tall, lanky man with a smile on his face. "You must be Pete Wasko," he said. "Come on in! You're right on time!"

On time? I checked my watch again. It said eight thirty! *Was I supposed to be here at eight or was it eight thirty?* All of a sudden my mind was in a state of mass chaos. I had no "Plan B." He turned and I followed him in like a little puppy following his master.

I stepped inside and looked around. Pastor Erb's family was sitting in the living room watching TV. One by one they greeted me. His warm friendly voice broke my stare. "Where would you like to sit and talk, Pete? My place is yours. Where would you be most comfortable?"

Still confused, I glared at him in silence as the anger started to return. Then I responded in an agitated voice, "This is not my house."

"Well," he replied, "let's go into the kitchen so we don't disturb anyone else."

We walked into the neatly arranged kitchen with an empty table except for the presence of a Bible lying in the middle. We sat down at the table.

"Your mother called me and told me a little bit about you," he said, then paused, using a bit of child psychology. He continued, "You know how mothers are, though. So why don't you tell me about yourself?"

I proceeded to spill out all the atrocities I had committed in Viet Nam and about all the things I'd done to get even with God, dating married women, cheating on my wife, the drugs and the alcohol.

He reached over and picked up the Bible from the table. Making direct eye contact with me he asked, "Pete, do you believe in this book? Do you believe in Jesus Christ?"

Of course, I believed in the Bible and Jesus! They had been an integral part of my whole life! Without breaking eye contact I sharply blurted out "Yes, I do,"

He opened the Bible to I John 1:9 and read, *"If we confess our sins, He is faithful and just to forgive our sin and to cleanse us from all unrighteousness."*

Feeling a little defensive I told him, "Look, I already told you that I believe every word in there."

Without missing a beat, he responded, "Then will you pray with me?"

Something was taking place inside me that I couldn't understand. In spite of all the drugs and the pint of Vodka in my system, my mind was calming. The adrenaline flow decreased. "I'll say the prayer," he continued. "All I need you to do is repeat the words after me."

After every phrase he spoke, I repeated his words, asking God to forgive me of all my sins. When we were finished he said to me "How do you feel now?"

I leaned forward and asked him "How do you want me to feel?"

He persisted "Do you feel any different?"

"Why would I feel any different?" I asked.

Then Pastor Erb explained, "Pete, because you prayed that prayer, God has forgiven you for all the wrong things you have done. You have a clean slate before God and now you can start building your life again!"

I started to laugh. "Listen, there's something you don't understand. God can do whatever He wants to. I believe He has forgiven me. However, He doesn't have to live inside of me and live with the things that I have done. I have to live in here." I pounded on the side of my head with my finger.

He leaned forward and looked me square in the eye and asked, "If God can forgive you and you can't, who are you? Are you greater than God?"

In an instant, as my mind searched for an answer, I realized I had put myself on the same plateau as God if not higher. I dropped my head and started bawling like a baby. A message entered my mind from somewhere beyond myself. *God has forgiven you and all the guilt of your past is gone.* I FELT the forgiveness of God. When I stopped crying I was completely straight. I didn't feel high from the drugs nor from the effects of the alcohol.

Pastor Erb advised, "One of the things you need to do is to create a new environment for yourself. You won't be able to hang out with your old friends or go to the bars to socialize. There's a place called The Barn. You need to go there on Thursday night at seven o'clock and make new friends. And you need to come to church on Sunday mornings. My church is Living Word Fellowship and we meet at the Bair Foundation building in New Wilmington." He handed me several tracts and said, "Here, read these. And start reading your Bible."

By the time I left his home about an hour or so later, I was excited! Bursting! I needed to share everything that happened to me in that brief time with someone, so I drove straight to my girlfriend's house. I knocked on her door and when she opened it, I said, "Come on and take a ride with me. I've got something to tell you. You'll never believe it."

As we drove around, I told her all about what had happened at Pastor Erb's home, how I had planned to kill the pastor because he was doing God's work and the change that had taken place inside me. I was certain she would be happy for me, but didn't get the response I'd expected.

"Throw all that stuff out," she said in disgust, glancing at the tracts that lay on the seat beside me. "It doesn't mean anything."

I continued to babble like a child. "But don't you understand? God forgave me. Everything I did in my past is gone! Gone! Don't you understand that?"

"But, Pete," she protested, "I don't think any of this is going to last. You feel good about it now, but who's to say you won't be back feeling the same old way tomorrow? Throw that stuff away."

I knew. I KNEW God had really done something special for me. I wasn't quite sure what, but I was sure that I could hardly wait to test it out. Later I realized that my girlfriend was afraid. She recognized that something had changed in my life and that being with her was a sin, but I hadn't realized it yet. I had a wife!

I'd never felt so good. After a short time of driving and talking we arrived back at her home. I told her good night and promised to call her later. Then I went home and waited with eagerness for my wife to get home from work.

After I told her my exciting experience, she responded in disgust, "Pete, you are who you are. There's no changing you."

I tried to get through to her how different I felt inside, but to no avail. In silence she turned away from me and went to bed.

That weekend I was on the straight and narrow. I informed all the kids I had supplied with drugs that I'd quit. "Jesus is the answer, guys," I explained. "He has a better 'high' for you than any drug you could ever take."

They were excited and accepted my invitation to the Barn Ministry on Thursday evening. But on Monday morning there I was right back to smoking marijuana and drinking alcohol. I began to think. *They're kids and I'm not. There's probably more hope for them than for me.*

I continued to use drugs the whole week, and never picked up my Bible or read any of the tracts that Pastor Erb had given me. Still, I continued to stay in contact with the kids, preaching to them that Jesus was the answer. I reminded them about The Barn and that I was supposed to go there on Thursday. We made plans to go together.

Thursday night came and so did the kids, knocking on my door. I was high on drugs but determined to get them to accept Jesus Christ as their Savior. We all piled into my car and headed for The Barn.

The Barn

I followed Pastor Erb's directions and ended up at a little metal building. As we walked in we saw people everywhere with their hands in the air, jumping and singing and praising God. They were praying in a language I couldn't understand. I walked into their midst and threw my hands into the air. *These are my kind of people!* They're partying! I thought to myself. I started singing and dancing right along with them without hesitation, I was so high I didn't realize what I was doing.

When praise and worship came to an end, Pastor Erb stood on the platform and asked everyone to sit down. We all did, but not in chairs. There were none, just some straw scattered on the floor. He taught for a while, but I have no idea what he preached about. Then he asked, "Does anyone here have a prayer need? If you do, stand up where you are and someone will pray with you."

I believe everyone who has made a commitment to the Lord struggles with their faith walk at some point in their early Christian life, and at other times, too. If we didn't, the enemy who wrestles with the decisions of our mind wouldn't be doing his job, would he? This was it for me, a time to test God. I prayed in silence, *If You are the God You claim to be, You'll heal my back.*

I stood up and closed my eyes. In moments I began to feel hands all over me and one exceptionally warm hand in the small of my back. I started shaking and vibrating all over. Uncontrollable tears flowed down my face. I listened to prayer after prayer on my behalf. After the praying ceased, I knew

God was the God He claimed to be. There was no pain at all in my back! I felt clean again, inside and out. Yes, I knew that I KNEW that God was real.

All the rest of the week and throughout the weekend I was clean, but that dreadful Monday was right around the corner to greet me. I returned the greeting. By smoking a joint! Yep, I started right back into drugs again.

Thursday came and, even though I was all buzzed up on speed and codeine, I planned to go to The Barn again. Instead my wife and I began to fight. I don't even remember what the fight was about, but it was a bad one. I had her backed against the wall and tempers were getting out of control. My cousin came in the door just in time to see what I was doing. She jumped on my back trying to disrupt my behavior.

When I realized my cousin was there, I released my hold on my wife and yelled, "I'd kill you, but you aren't worth spending the rest of my life in jail! I'm going to The Barn, and when I come back I'm leaving you. All I want is my car, my Harley Davidson motorcycle, and a couple of bucks to see me through."

"Where will you go?" she retorted.

"I have no idea," I told her, "but I know I'm NOT coming back here to be with you!" I stormed out of the house, got in my car and went to pick up a few of the kids who I'd invited to go to The Barn with me.

We arrived there early enough to get seats in the front row. Soon the place was filled with people. Pastor Erb walked to the front and introduced a guest speaker, Reverend Dick Burns. I was irritated. *I don't want to hear that guy! I don't want to hear anyone except Pastor Erb.*

But as this man spoke, I felt as though he was speaking right to me. He talked about the mess we make of our lives by the decisions we make. That was me, all right! He followed his message with an altar call. "If you were to leave this earth tonight, do you know where you would go?"

I began to think, *I don't even have any idea where I'm going when I leave this place. Florida? California? I have no idea. All I know is I'm NOT going home!* I stood to respond to the altar call, intending to pray for direction on where I should go when I left The Barn that night. Reaching the front, I kneeled. When Reverend Burns laid both of his hands on the top of my head I felt as though a lightning bolt hit me, a light so bright the naked eye would never be able to stand it. My whole body began to shake. The next thing I knew, I was praying in that strange language I'd heard others pray that first night. As my body continued to vibrate, I began to cry. By the time I left The Barn that night, I was completely straight again, and on fire for God. I couldn't believe I was straight again. It felt so good! (Straight means no longer feeling the effects of the drugs and/or alcohol, so that you are making decisions without their influence.)

I went back home to tell my wife what had happened, and apologized to her for all the times I had mistreated her. I grabbed all my drugs and held them out for her to see, then flushed them down the toilet.

Not long after that, I returned to the cemetery where my father was buried and prayed, "Lord, please forgive him. You forgave me for all the wrongs I've done. Now please forgive my father. I'm sure he's in hell, but, please, if you can, bring him out."

I heard a voice say, "What makes you think he's in hell? Who made you the Judge?"

For the next ten months I had no desire to drink or do drugs and I attended church and Bible studies on a regular basis.

Years later, in 1988, while I was in the middle of a forty-day fast, I drove to Pleasant Valley Church in Niles, Ohio, to listen to a speaker named Dave Reaver, a born again Viet Nam vet. During the worship I heard my father singing and looked all around. It had to be Dad! I'd recognize his voice anywhere! Reassurance flooded my whole being. HE'S OKAY!

> *Day by day in every way through the grace of God I am getting better and better.*

April 1969

Gary Johnson from Moss Point, Mississippi. Gary was the first man that tended to my aide when I hit the first land mine on Dec. 21, 1968. This photo was taken in April, 1969 in Viet Nam.

No Coincidence

One day my aunt phoned. Her aunt was in the hospital and she wanted me to go and pray for her. I told her I would.

"There's one big obstacle, Pete," she warned. "Her sons will be there and they don't believe in born again Christians."

A challenge! My goal was to get past them. No big deal! I prayed the whole way to the hospital, and by the time I got there I had a peace about me that couldn't be shaken. I trusted God to get me past them.

As I pulled into the hospital parking lot, my vehicle had a flat tire. I thought, *Great! Now I have to fix this before I go in!* I changed the tire and then entered the hospital to look for a place to wash my dirty hands. As I walked in, two guys walked out. Laughing, I held my palms out for them to see and said, "Look at this, try to go visit someone in the hospital and you get a flat tire!"

They directed me to the bathroom then left. I washed my hands and located the room where I needed to be. Her sons were not there so I kneeled by her bed and started praying. In a soft voice, the patient in the bed said, "You're Dolores' son Pete, aren't you?"

I was amazed. Although I had never met the lady before, I'd been told she was in and out of consciousness and saying over and over, "I don't want to die. I'm afraid to die." But she talked to me!

She explained, "God told me you were coming to see me. I'm not scared anymore." I sat in the chair beside her bed and continued to pray and talk with her.

Without warning, her sons entered the room, the same two guys who had told me where the bathroom was. They were upset to see me in their mother's room. "Who are you?" one of them demanded. "Why are you here?"

They were astounded when their mother looked up and said, "We're talking." Their protest ended.

A few months after that incident that dear lady died. Her sons thanked me for going to see her because they knew it had helped her experience a peaceful death. I was in awe to think that God had told someone who was in and out of consciousness that I was on my way to see her. At that moment I realized God had a greater hand in my life than I thought.

Even though I had turned my life over to the Lord and believed I was "doing it right," my relationship with my wife was not good. The hurts from the past were too deep; the trust level was nearly zero. I didn't follow Pastor Erb's advice to make new friends. My old buddies continued to encourage me to have a drink every now and then. The drinking led me back to doing drugs. Then it was the old girlfriend thing again.

I went on a fishing trip to the ocean with my wife's father and family. When I returned home, the house we'd made our home for only forty five days was nearly empty. She'd left me and taken my son as well.

My abuse of alcohol and drugs increased, but there was a difference. Every time I took a drink I looked in the bottom of the bottle and saw myself with a spike in one hand and a hammer in the other. I was hammering Jesus' hand to the cross. The mental pain was nearly unbearable. After all Jesus had done for me and there I was, back to my old ways.

As a man thinketh in his heart so is he.

VI

A CHANCE TO START OVER

One night as I continued to hit the bars, drinking and doing drugs, I walked into a little restaurant/bar called Quaker Steak and Lube in Sharon, Pennsylvania. As I crossed the room to the bar, I heard a voice from the other side of the room call out, "Hey, Pete Wasko! Come and do some shots with us."

To my amazement, it was Carla Cline. I had gone to high school with her, but hadn't seen her in ten years. Carla, petite and dark haired and friendly as always, was with a friend who was separated from her husband, but the husband was there. He called me over and asked me to take Carla home so he and his wife could talk and try to work things out between them.

As I drove Carla home, I confessed how wrong I was for doing drugs and drinking since I had turned my life over to the Lord. I told her about the prayer meetings I'd been attending at The Barn and a Catholic church.

Surprised, she said, "My mom goes to those meetings at the Catholic church! You and Mom would get along well. You're both hypocrites."

Her cutting remark never even fazed me. I just continued to talk and talk. As we pulled up in front of her home, she commented, "Thank God I'm home! There's nothing worse than a drunken Jesus freak!"

For the next three weeks I couldn't get Carla off my mind. I phoned her daily, but she refused to talk to me. She wouldn't even answer the phone.

I couldn't get the fact out of my mind that I continued to sin and backslide against God. This thought convicted me without mercy. Every day after work I tried to drown these convicting thoughts and mental pictures by going out drinking until I passed out. I wanted to get rid of that picture at the bottom of my drinking glass of Christ's hand nailed to the cross by me. One day while at the car dealership where I was selling cars, the thought ran through my head, Tonight I will get rid of that picture once and forever, no matter what I have to do.

About five minutes before I was to leave work, one of the other salesmen came up to me and said, "There's a young lady outside looking for you."

I walked outside and there was Carla sitting in her blue Camaro. "Where have you been?" she asked.

"What are you talking about? I've been calling you on the phone for three weeks without any luck at all and now you show up where I work and ask me where have I been?"

Carla laughed. Filled with enthusiasm she said "I started going to those prayer meetings at the Catholic Church and I've turned my life over to the Lord, but I haven't seen you there. You need to start going again.

"You're right," I confessed. "I know I need to go back. They really helped,"

Carla said," Why don't you get in my car with me and we will go to the Red Barn restaurant? My family is there now. It's my daughter's birthday and we're getting something to eat." I accepted her invitation, went to the restaurant with her and met her daughter and family.

The following week we started hanging out together and going to the prayer meeting. She knew I was trying to talk my wife into returning home and gave me ideas that might help sway my wife's decision to return to me. We tried everything we could come up with but I had hurt my wife too deeply and too often. She'd had enough and was closed to my offers, since in the past they had always been empty promises. Our marriage ended in divorce.

In October, 1977, Carla and I started dating, but we didn't have your average relationship. We emptied our mental closets and shared all the sins of our past with each other so there would be no surprises. I told her everything and she told me everything. I mean EVERTHING: Viet Nam, my extramarital affairs, the drugs and alcohol, the mental hospital and my daughter that no one knew about. She told me about her two previous marriages, her being raped at gun point, all her bad childhood experiences and her extramarital experiences. When we were done, we knew about all the dirt in each others' lives. We also shared all our past hurts from childhood to the present day. At the time, we didn't realize the freedom this sharing brought to our relationship. We both knew there was nothing in our past that could come up and cause division between us. Another great benefit from our openness with each other was the fact that we accepted each other regardless of the other's past, and we could look at each other without bringing up what had gone on before in a negative way.

In January, 1978 Carla and I made our commitment to God and each other in marriage and six months later I adopted her eight–year-old daughter Laurie.

> *"Talk the way you would like to be and you will be the way you talk."*

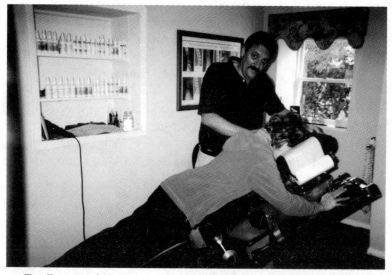

Dr. Pete working on a patient, fulfilling his childhood dream!

Blessings From Above

The story of adopting Laurie is another testimony of God at work in Carla's life as well as in mine. When I returned from Viet Nam I was stationed at Fort Knox, Kentucky. On most weekends I returned home and stayed with a married woman who was separated from her husband. However, I never let my family know I was in town. Well, one weekend I came home sober and feeling guilty for not stopping at my mother's house. (Being "self-medicated" with alcohol also removed all those guilty feelings.) My mother was excited to see me and asked me what type blood I had because my cousin Kathleen, a type one diabetic, was in labor and needed people to be at the hospital in case she needed blood. Well, I had the same type blood, so I went to the hospital.

I spent the entire weekend at the hospital with my cousin's family which was also my family and with the relatives of her best friend who was in labor at the same time. They both gave birth that weekend. Her best friend happened to be Carla, and it was her daughter Laurie who was born that day. Eight years later I adopted her. God had arranged for me to be there the day she was born!

Today, Laurie has two children of her own, a girl and a boy. She has been blessed with the ability to organize and is a valuable helper in our business. She also has her own cleaning business called Squeaky Clean.

Eighteen months after Carla and I married, July 10, 1979, our son Jason was born into our family. Born with a birth defect Jason has undergone two reconstructive surgeries on his chest. I used to wonder if the defect was caused by my drug and alcohol abuse, but today it doesn't matter. God is faithful and our son is fine. He has been given several gifts from God and one is a beautiful voice. While in high school he won the all state singing competitions three years in a row. Today, he is a hair stylist with a promising career.

On May 26, 1983 our daughter Jessica was born in spite of my having a vasectomy a year and a half earlier. I had a lot of problems after my surgery and we found out why. God wasn't done blessing us with children. We named her Jessica because it means "Gift of God". She is also a hair stylist with a promising career.

My first son Pete is married with a beautiful wife Megan, and has two sons. He is in his final year of a five year electrical apprenticeship program and is gifted with a mechanical and electrical ability to work and fix almost anything. I am not so blessed in that area, so he is a big help in many ways.

My firstborn daughter and I are just getting to know each other. Almost two years ago I was able to locate her and tell her I was her biological father. She is married with three children.

What you say is what you get.

Marriage by God

Today, nearly twenty eight years after our marriage, Carla and I both continue to walk with Christ, free from the bondage of drugs, alcohol and our past. As I look back on my journey with God, I must admit, yes, it was a rocky road and a trying time for both of us. We've come close to divorce, but made the decision to remain true to our commitment to one another, our children and more importantly to our marriage vows made before God. We are both aware of the ripples we could cause in the pond of our lives, the lives of our children, our family and our friends if we allowed our thoughts to control us instead of us getting our thoughts under control. If we hadn't, we would have ended up in divorce court. We've never regretted standing firm and working and praying through the tough times rather than giving up and walking away.

My wife, Carla, deserves a medal of some kind. She has weathered the horror of my past flashbacks, nightmares and mood swings that were the product of my experiences in the Viet Nam war. I want to share a flashback and a recurring nightmare with you to demonstrate that there is hope for individuals to gain control over these debilitating psychological experiences. My wife's choice to stick by my side when times were really tough has caused both of us to grow stronger.

We were always moving. At one time we moved every six months for three years. I was running away from something but I didn't know what it was. I didn't realize that I was running away from my past and myself. I had forgotten who I was before the war, before all of the mental and physical trauma. I had lost touch with reality and didn't know where to find it or myself. Consciously I was acting out the confused mental turmoil that was going on in my subconscious mind. My subconscious thoughts had become my reality.

On June 21, 1987, we had just moved from our home in Sharpsville, Pa to New Wilmington, Pa. It was getting close to the Fourth of July, a holiday I am glad to see come to an end. Fireworks and stuff, ya know! After we had been in bed for approximately two hours, I woke up and got out of bed. I checked the kids to see if they were alright, looked out the windows and lay down on the couch to sleep for the next two hours. Mentally and emotionally I was still pulling guard duty. I had been doing it for so long it had become normal to me.

I had just fallen asleep when I heard motorcycles and explosions outside of the house. I jumped to my feet and looked out the window. My distorted mind interpreted what I saw and heard as gunfire coming toward my home. Our home was the first house on the right entering a cul-de-sac that had only five homes on it, so I knew their only way out was to go past our house again. When they approached my home on their way out, I was standing in the middle of the road in my shorts with a rifle in one hand and a knife in the other. What I thought was a motorcycle gang ended up being two boys on a four wheeler. When they saw me standing there they screamed and turned into the field opposite my house. I pulled the rifle up and started shooting at them as they drove into the darkness. Calmly I walked into the house and into the bedroom. My wife, visibly upset, asked me, "Pete, what are you doing?"

"I'm just protecting what's mine," I replied, then went back to the couch and entered a peaceful rest knowing that the intruders would not be back.

The next morning my wife asked me to call our church and set up a counseling session with our Associate Pastor Roger Aiello who had helped me get through some other really tough times. "Why?" I asked.

"What you did last night was not normal. You still need some help."

I explained, "But it's my responsibility as a man to protect my family and home."

She continued to argue with me over the matter. Three days later, as I was bent over tying my shoes before leaving for work, I lifted my head, looked at her and said "What I did the other night was so wrong! I could have crippled or even killed one of those kids. They were just out having fun the way I used to do around the Fourth of July holiday when I was a kid."

This had been a bad flashback! I called the church and set the appointment.

In a nightmare I experienced many times, I'm standing in the middle of a room up to my waist in blood and body parts. I'm turning my head to the left then the right as I grab pieces of arms, legs and other fragmented parts of human bodies. I stuff them into a black body bag, trying to hide them so no one will discover what I've done. However, I'm crying hysterically knowing I will never be able to get all the body parts into the bag and get the place cleaned up. It is useless, but I MUST keep trying. I start to lose it mentally. *I know they'll find them. What am I going to do with them? I have to work harder and faster! Come on Pete hurry, hurry!* Then I wake up sweating, shaking and crying. It took hours to get myself under control.

For years after returning from Viet Nam, this was one of the very disturbing and unexplainable nightmares that I experienced on a regular basis. However, thirty three years later, the cause of this puzzling and upsetting nightmare was brought to light one evening during a phone call. I was talking to the driver of the track I was on when I hit the landmine in February, 1969. This was the first time I had talked to him since I left Viet Nam thirty three years earlier. I said to him "Wasn't it just a miracle that none of us were killed when we hit the landmine?"

He replied, "That's not exactly true, Pete. After the initial explosion of the landmine under our track, I was lying on the ground as they tended to me and the other wounded soldiers. They were also waiting for the track to stop exploding so they could put the fire out because the track was also burning. Pete, we knew you didn't make it because you were still inside the exploding track. They were waiting to pick up your remains if there were any left."

My driver then told me that as he glanced toward the site he saw me crawling around in the body parts of the one of the gunners inside the burning inferno. As I found my way out of the furnace of death, a couple men ran to the fiery border and dragged me to safety. No wonder I was tormented by the re-occurring nightmare about stuffing body parts in a black bag!

Every time I stood crying and shaken beyond control after one of my nightmares, Carla would stand in front of me saying "Come on Pete. Come back, Pete. You can do this. With God all things are possible. Come on Pete— you can do it." She continued to speak words of encouragement to me until I calmed down. My wife had faith in me when I didn't. She saw possibility and potential in me that neither I nor anyone else could see.

God has touched my life in a way that leaves no doubt that where I am today is a miracle. The fact we are still to-gether is a miracle. The main reason is because of our commit-ment to God. Today, our marriage is stronger than it has ever been. We realize for anything to grow and become better it takes work and an unwavering commitment. Daily, through prayer and honest communication, we work at our relation-ship with God and our marriage because we want the best relationship possible with our Creator and each other. We want and strive for the best because, what else is there?

Talk your way forward.

VII
IT CAN HAPPEN TO YOU

Are you living your dream life? Are your relationships with those closest to you the way you want them to be? If not, I want you to realize that it is possible. I want you to know that it doesn't matter where your previous bad choices in life have put you or what you have done up to this very moment. What really matters is, What you are going to do with your life now? I believe that if you follow the same truths I followed to get where I am, you can reach your desires as well!

My life journey made a "right" turn the night I made the decision to live my life for Jesus Christ. Until that time I had accepted my life of sin as normal. I was entangled in sin for so long that drinking, drugs, sexual immorality and fighting became an acceptable lifestyle. I FELT free and okay, but didn't realize I was in bondage. I wasn't free at all! I was not aware of the fact that every decision I made reaped consequences. I didn't realize that my wrongdoings would affect me and so many others in a negative way for years to come.

When I confessed my sins to God, asked Him to forgive me, and accepted Jesus as my Lord and Savior, I KNEW He had given me a chance to start over. A chance to make my dreams come true! He gave me an opportunity to live a new kind of life without any excuses from the past to stop me. I was forgiven and free from all the guilt and shame that had caused me to lose all respect for myself and for others. However, the most exciting part was that now I had a Helper. I had the presence of God's Holy Spirit to lead, guide, and strengthen me along the way.

Every day I read the Bible to find out how God wants me to live in order to bring peace and joy into my life. I found the secret to living a better life in this book. In fact, the day I read in His word that He knew me before He'd formed me in the womb of my mother and already had a plan for me I got excited!

I reasoned to myself, "If He knew me before He sent me here and if He had a plan for my life before I got here I wanted and needed to know what that plan was."

You are no different than I am. He has a plan for you too. His plan is to give you a future and a hope.

Part of that plan includes getting to know your heavenly Father. I had always wanted to know my earthly father, but that was not possible. Now I had the chance to experience a father son relationship with my heavenly Father, and I jumped at the opportunity. So I spent time finding out everything I could about Him. I spent a lot of time talking to Him, and asking Him for strength and direction. I got to know my heavenly Father in a very real way.

In the process of reading His Word I discovered I am not to be conformed to this world, but I am to be transformed by the renewing of my mind. I also learned that if I took every thought captive to the obedience of Christ, I would not only renew my mind, but I could also destroy all my old thought patterns that I had raised up against Him to justify my life of sin.

These thoughts always came to my mind while I tried to make decisions and they caused a lot of confusion. So I went to a Christian counselor and to the Bible to grasp a clearer understanding of Bible principles and how I should apply them to my life. Yes, I asked for help. I swallowed my pride because I wanted everything God had for me in His plan.

I also became a member of a Bible believing and Bible preaching church. I took every class the church had to offer in order to learn and grow into the person God had intended for me to become. To this day I am still taking classes for personal growth and a deeper understanding of my Lord.

One day, after sharing my testimony with some prisoners at a halfway house, I began to thank God for putting me in a situation where I could share what He had done for me. I felt that God responded, "Pete, you have it all right except one thing. ... I couldn't have done it without you."

See, God is not looking for puppets; He is looking for willing vessels. He is looking for you! He wants His plans for your life to come to pass. He wants to give you a testimony to share with others.

Today I am living my childhood dream of becoming a doctor. I am Dr. Pete Wasko and have been a practicing chiropractor for nine years, eight of those years in New Wilmington, Pa. My wife and I are blessed with a successful practice, a health food store, and an apartment building where our practice is located. I am blessed with a beautiful marriage. And now that this book is published, I can add "author" to that list of blessings. That was another one of my dreams.

My prayer today is that you will make the changes necessary for beginning your journey toward living your dream. Your journey starts the moment you decide what you really want out of life. Then make an unwavering commitment to God and allow Him to guide, encourage and strengthen you. Allow Him to teach you how to change and to do all that is necessary for the fulfillment of your dream. Remember, ALL things are possible to him that believes, and NEVER, NEVER, NEVER, NEVER give up.

If You Don't Like The Way Your Life Is...

CHANGE IT!

Dr. Pete Wasko was in sales from age twenty-six to forty-one, rising to Regional Vice President with an insurance/investment firm, and to general sales manager of a car dealership. He also owned a fire and burglar alarm business. In 1988 Dr. Pete went through extensive

Dr. Pete and wife Carla.

training in personality profiling (Behavioral Style Analysis).

In 1991 Dr. Pete left his sales career to pursue his lifelong aspiration of becoming a doctor. In 1996 he graduated as a Doctor of Chiropractic, fulfilling his dream. Dr. Pete Wasko speaks at churches, prisons, business meetings, public schools, military installations, Christian television talk shows, radio programs and youth groups. His School of Health, which is a free monthly school to educate the public about their health concerns, has been running since 2002.

In 1999 he and his wife Carla were ordained as ministers after attending Christian Life School of Theology and serving as elders for several years.

Dr. Wasko has also written a ten hour class on Ruling Your Spirit (mind). This course was designed to help individuals bring their thoughts and life under control and to help them become the best they can be in their careers, their relationships, or in any other endeavor.

Dr. Wasko is available for motivational and inspirational speaking engagements that can enhance not only an individual's personal life, but also increase church and/or business growth.

You can contact Dr. Pete at *drpeterj@adelphia.net* or at 210 West Neshannock Ave. New Wilmington, PA 16142.